my

NATIONAL GEOGRAPHIC KiDS

weird but true!

Fact-a-Day FUN Journal

NATIONAL GEOGRAPHIC
WASHINGTON, D.C.

Visit us online:
Kids: kids.nationalgeographic.com
Parents: nationalgeographic.com/books
Teachers: ngchildrensbooks.org
Librarians: ngchildrensbooks.org

For information about special discounts for bulk purchases, please contact National Geographic Books
Special Sales: ngspecsales@ngs.org
For rights or permissions inquiries, please contact National Geographic Books
Subsidiary Rights: ngbookrights@ngs.org

Hardcover ISBN: 978-1-4263-1727-9

Printed in Hong Kong
14/THK/1

my
weird but True
365

What are the **WEIRDEST TIMES** of the year? Record them **ALL HERE!**

NAME ....

BIRTHDAY ....

AGE .... Years .... Months .... Hours

WEIRDEST TIME OF DAY ....

WEIRDEST WAY TO SPEND THE DAY ....

WEIRDEST DAY OF THE WEEK ....

WEIRDEST DAY OF THE YEAR ....

WEIRDEST MONTH ....

WEIRDEST HOLIDAY ....

WEIRDEST SEASON ....

WEIRDEST FAMILY TRADITIONS AND CELEBRATIONS ....

5

JANUARY

1

THE NEW YEAR'S BALL IN TIMES SQUARE ALMOST WEIGHS 12,000 POUNDS. (5,450 kg)

▶ What's the **FUNNIEST THING** you've ever done to **RING IN THE NEW YEAR?**

Scream happy new year

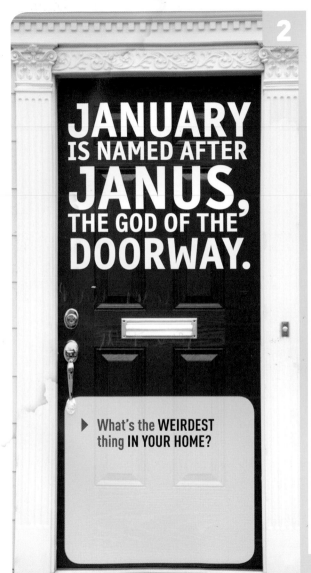

JANUARY IS NAMED AFTER JANUS, THE GOD OF THE DOORWAY.

▶ What's the WEIRDEST thing IN YOUR HOME?

2

IN THE 18TH CENTURY, FRUITCAKES WERE BANNED IN EUROPE.

▶ HOW FAR can you FLING your leftover fruitcake? (Ask a parent for permission to try this outside.)

3

4

This animal is called a CARIBOU in North America, and a REINDEER in Europe.

▶ If you could change YOUR NAME, what would you CHANGE IT TO?

5

PIEGNARTOQ
MEANS
"THE SNOW THAT IS GOOD
FOR DRIVING SLED"
IN THE INUIT
LANGUAGE.

7

MOST
SNOWFLAKES
ARE SIX-SIDED.

6

CHIONOPHOBIA
IS THE FEAR OF SNOW.

10

▶ If you could make a crazy **SNOW SCULPTURE,** what would it be?

a house

ELVIS PRESLEY LOVED FRIED **PEANUT BUTTER** AND **BANANA SANDWICHES.**

▶ What's the **STRANGEST SANDWICH** you've ever eaten?

9

January

is the 3,265th most popular GIRL'S NAME in the UNITED STATES.

▶ What's the most common
GIRL'S NAME at your school?

10

A MALE POLAR BEAR
CAN GROW TO BE

10

FEET (3 m)
TALL

—THAT'S AS TALL AS A
ONE-STORY BUILDING.

▶ QUIZ! HOW BIG was the
biggest animal YOU'VE
ever seen?

A. smaller than a
backpack
B. bigger than a car
C. as big as a table

The original ROMAN CALENDAR had only 304 DAYS.

▶ Draw a picture of yourself as a citizen of **ANCIENT ROME** here.

12

A SNOWSHOE HARE CAN **HOP UP TO 30 MILES**........ **AN HOUR.**
(48 kph)

▶ If you could have a **SUPERPOWER,** what would it be?

TODAY IS

NATIONAL RUBBER DUCKY DAY

The world's largest
RUBBER DUCKY is 40 feet tall.
(12 m)

▶ "What time does a duck wake up? At the quack of dawn!" **MAKE UP** your own **DUCK JOKE.**

14

TODAY IS · NATIONAL DRESS UP YOUR PET DAY

AMERICANS SPEND **$61 BILLION** ON THEIR PETS EACH YEAR.

▶ Place a funny **PET PICTURE** here.

15

HAPPY BIRTHDAY · MARTIN LUTHER KING, JR.

MARTIN LUTHER KING, JR.—who gave the famous "I Have a Dream" speech—ONCE RECEIVED A C IN A PUBLIC SPEAKING COURSE.

▶ What's **YOUR** secret **TALENT?**

16

TODAY IS — NATIONAL NOTHING DAY

THE FIRST EVIDENCE OF THE USE OF ZERO IS OVER **4,000** YEARS OLD.

▶ Can you make a list of **FIVE WACKY WAYS** to **DO NOTHING?**

17

A SNOWY OWL GETS *WHITER* AS IT GETS *OLDER.*

▶ **QUIZ! How tall is the BIGGEST SNOWMAN you've ever built?**

A. as tall as a dog
B. as tall as a car
C. as tall as your parents
D. as tall as a dinosaur
E. I've never built a snowman.

18

A SNOW LEOPARD CAN LEAP AS FAR AS 50 FEET (15 m)—THAT'S LONGER THAN THE *LENGTH OF A SCHOOL BUS.*

19

SNOW MONKEYS HAVE BEEN KNOWN TO MAKE *SNOWBALLS FOR FUN.*

Sculptors made a **FULL-SIZE** castle out of ice at a festival in China.

▶ If you were to carve the world's **GREATEST** ice sculpture, what would be **YOUR SUBJECT?**

21

TODAY IS

SQUIRREL APPRECIATION DAY

Squirrels often FORGET where they HIDE THEIR ACORNS.

▶ What do you have **SQUIRRELED AWAY** in your room?

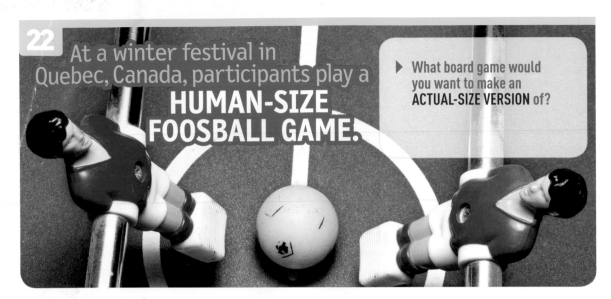

22

At a winter festival in Quebec, Canada, participants play a **HUMAN-SIZE FOOSBALL GAME.**

▶ What board game would you want to make an **ACTUAL-SIZE VERSION** of?

23

TODAY IS — NATIONAL HANDWRITING DAY

Graphophobia is the fear of handwriting.

▶ Write your name a **DIFFERENT WAY** here.

24

Bears that live in warmer climates don't hibernate because it's possible to find food year-round.

▶ What's the LONGEST you've EVER SLEPT?

25

THE FIRST SNOWSHOES WERE USED MORE THAN 6,000 YEARS AGO.

▶ Describe the **GOOFIEST PAIR** of shoes you've ever worn.

26

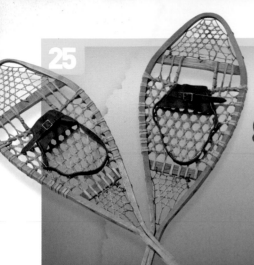

TODAY IS AUSTRALIA DAY

THERE'S AN ANNUAL COCKROACH RACE IN BRISBANE, AUSTRALIA.

▶ What **ANIMAL** would you like to see **IN A RACE?**

27

King Henry III *had a pet polar bear.*

▶ If you could have any **ANIMAL** as a **PET,** what would it be?

25

TODAY IS

NATIONAL BUBBLE WRAP APPRECIATION DAY

Bubble Wrap

was originally sold as

wallpaper.

▶ How many Bubble Wrap bubbles can **YOU POP** in 30 seconds?

An inch of rain (2.5 cm)

IS EQUAL TO

10 inches

(25 cm) of snow.

▶ What's the **DEEPEST SNOWFALL** you've ever seen?

30

HOT CHOCOLATE
was invented by the Maya thousands of years ago.

▶ What **NEW CHOCOLATE TREAT** would you invent?

The fastest backward mile (1.6 km) was run in six minutes two seconds.

▶ Write your **FAVORITE SONG** title **BACKWARD** here.

FEBRUARY

GARLIC

▶ What **STINKY FOODS** are your favorites? List them here and describe their **FUNKY SMELLS.**

1

PEOPLE IN FLORIDA, U.S.A., CELEBRATE A FESTIVAL EACH FEBRUARY.

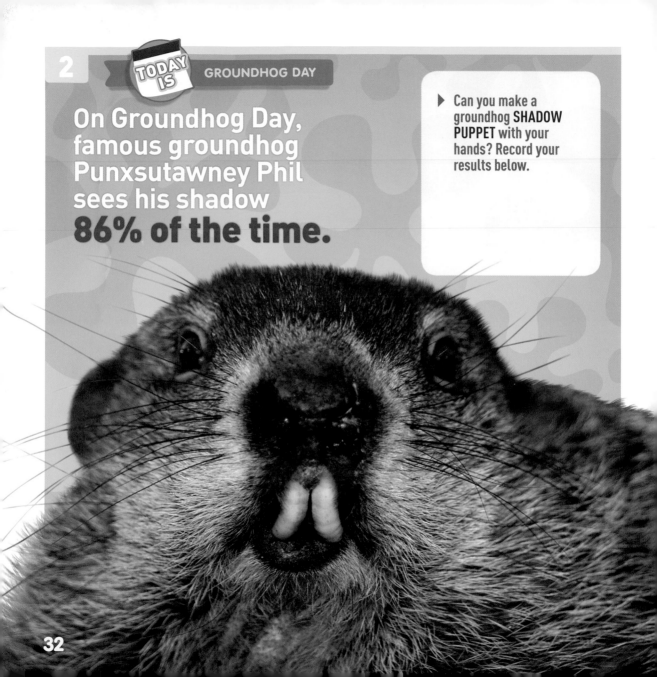

TODAY IS   GROUNDHOG DAY

On Groundhog Day, famous groundhog Punxsutawney Phil sees his shadow **86% of the time.**

▶ Can you make a groundhog **SHADOW PUPPET** with your hands? Record your results below.

3

February is LIBRARY LOVERS month.

▶ Jumble up the titles of your three **FAVORITE BOOKS** to create a **NEW WACKY TITLE.**

4

▶ Draw a picture of you **KNIGHTING A PENGUIN.**

Norway once knighted a penguin named Sir Nils Olav.

5

Penguins remove salt from the water they drink by sneezing.

▶ What **FUNNY THINGS** make you **SNEEZE?**

6

1,250,000,000 pounds (566,990,500 kg)
of chicken wings are sold on Super Bowl weekend.

THE SHORTEST SUPER BOWL COMMERCIAL WAS ONLY A HALF SECOND LONG.

▶ What's the **WEIRDEST SNACK FOOD** you eat?

▶ **TRY SAYING** more than one word in half a second. **CAN YOU?**

7

8

If you could pick **SIX ACTIVITIES** for your **OWN OLYMPICS,** what would you choose?

The first Winter Olympics was held in 1924 and featured only six sports.

9

Painting was once an Olympic sport.

▶ Combine two of your favorite activities to create **A NEW OLYMPIC SPORT.** (Dance-knitting? Skateboard-singing?)

10

For good luck, medieval soldiers carried purple amethysts, February's birthstone, to PROTECT THEM IN BATTLE.

▶ Do you have any strange GOOD LUCK CHARMS?

37

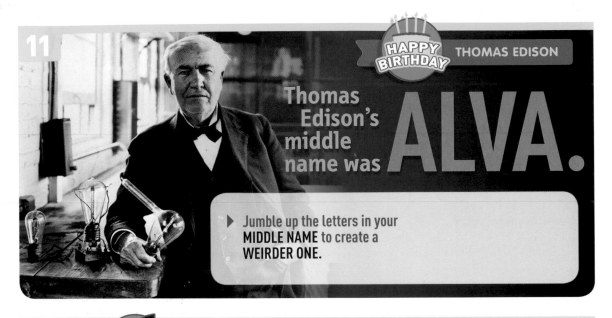

11

Thomas Edison's middle name was **ALVA.**

▶ Jumble up the letters in your **MIDDLE NAME** to create a **WEIRDER ONE.**

12

TODAY IS · NATIONAL PANCAKE DAY

Women in Kansas, U.S.A., and England celebrate National Pancake Day by running in a race and **FLIPPING PANCAKES.**

▶ Think of **FIVE OTHER USES** for **PANCAKES** and write them here.

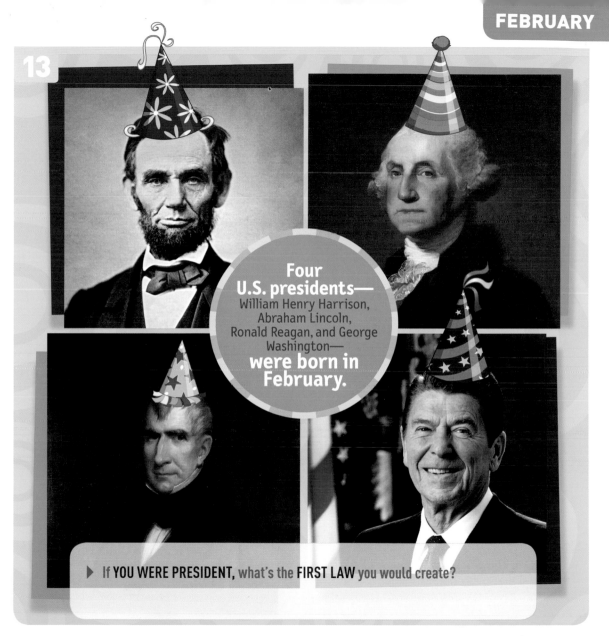

13

Four
U.S. presidents—
William Henry Harrison,
Abraham Lincoln,
Ronald Reagan, and George
Washington—
were born in
February.

▶ If **YOU WERE PRESIDENT,** what's the **FIRST LAW** you would create?

14

ENOUGH CANDY HEARTS ARE SOLD FOR
Valentine's Day
TO REACH FROM
Arizona, U.S.A., to Italy
MORE THAN 20 TIMES.

▶ Draw a picture of **YOUR VALENTINE** here.

15

YOUR HEART PUMPS
2,000 gallons
(7,570 L)
OF BLOOD THROUGH YOUR BODY PER DAY— THAT'S MORE
THAN 40 bathtubs' worth of blood.

▶ How many times does your **HEART BEAT** in ten seconds? (Do 25 jumping jacks and count again!)

Abraham Lincoln is listed in the **NATIONAL WRESTLING HALL OF FAME.**

▶ What **HALL OF FAME** could you be listed in?

17 In North Cape, Norway, the SUN DOESN'T SET in winter for one full month.

▶ What WOULD YOU DO if the sun were STILL UP AT 3 A.M.?

18 It is possible for it to SNOW WITHOUT any CLOUDS in the sky.

▶ What's the WEIRDEST WEATHER day you can remember?

▶ What's the **BIGGEST STRUCTURE** you can build **WITH ICE CUBES** before they melt? Draw a picture of your creation here.

19 **Icebergs can be as small as ICE CUBES or as big as SOME COUNTRIES.**

TODAY IS

NATIONAL LOVE YOUR PET DAY

164 MILLION dogs and cats live in homes in the United States. That's almost 1 pet for every 2 people!

▶ Imagine the **GREATEST PET** of all time and **DRAW IT** here.

21

In Old English, February was called Kalemonath or **"cabbage month."**

▶ If you could give **FEBRUARY A DIFFERENT NAME,** what would it be?

George Washington's favorite food was ice cream.

▶ In some places you can order **PICKLE OR OYSTER ICE CREAM.** What kind of ice cream would you invent?

23

THE INVENTOR OF THE
snow cone machine
SERVED HIS CREATIONS AT EVERY TEXAS, U.S.A., STATE FAIR FOR 65 YEARS.

▶ What's your **FAVORITE FROZEN TREAT?**

Each February at the **BATTLE OF THE ORANGES** festival in Ivrea, Italy, residents throw over **400 TONS OF ORANGES** at each other. (363 mT)

▶ How many **ORANGES** can you **JUGGLE** at one time?

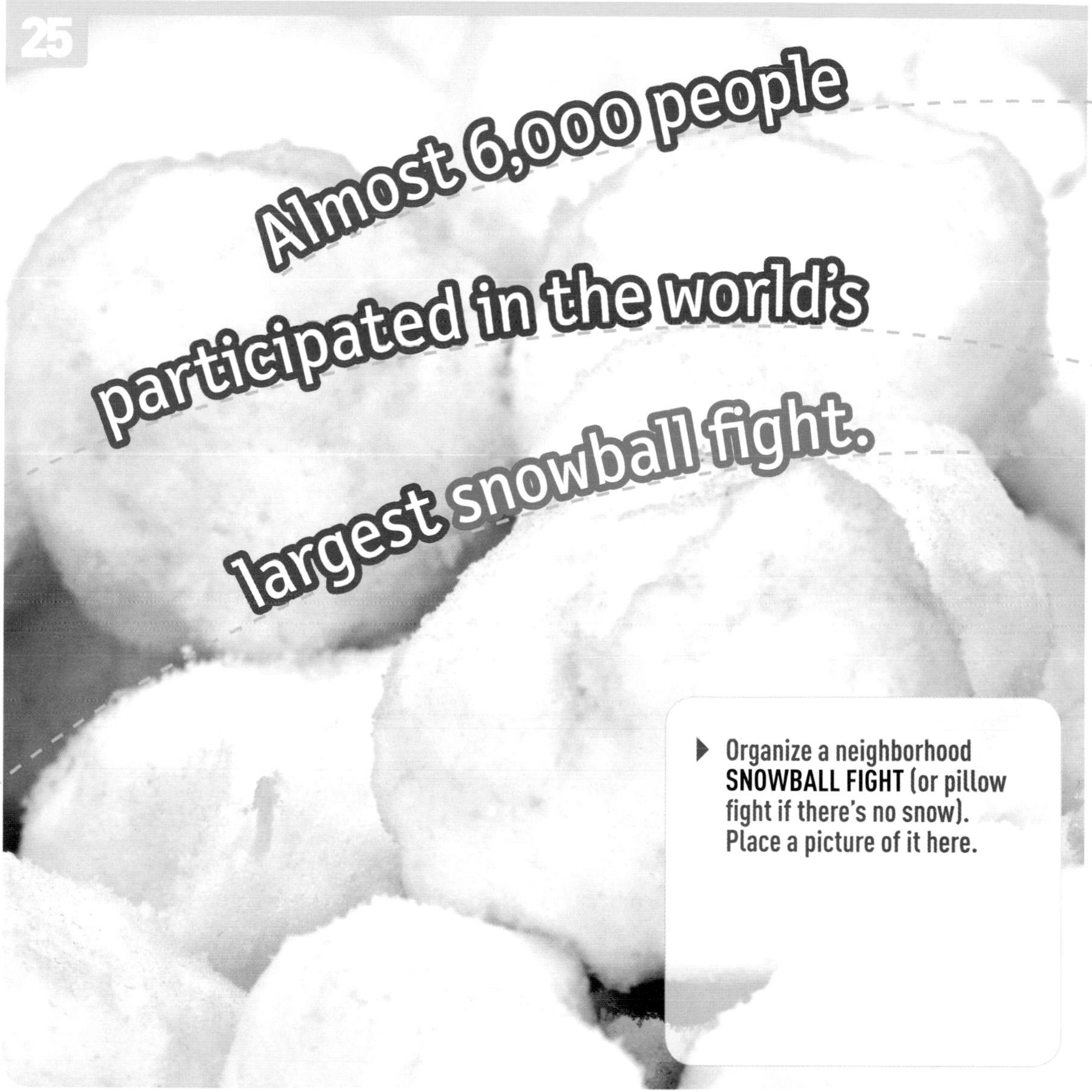

25

Almost 6,000 people participated in the world's largest snowball fight.

▶ Organize a neighborhood **SNOWBALL FIGHT** (or pillow fight if there's no snow). Place a picture of it here.

TODAY IS TELL A FAIRY TALE DAY

IN THE ORIGINAL VERSION OF "THE FROG PRINCE," THE PRINCESS DOESN'T KISS THE FROG. SHE BREAKS THE SPELL BY SLAMMING HIM AGAINST A WALL.

▶ Finish this sentence: "ONCE UPON A TIME _____."

27

A MAN ONCE DROVE A ZAMBONI ALL THE WAY ACROSS CANADA.

▶ Walk by placing **ONE FOOT** directly **IN FRONT OF THE OTHER** so that your feet touch. How many steps does it take to get all the way across your bedroom?

OLYMPIA

Leap years, when February has 29 days, only occur that are divisible

▶ Do the math! Is **THIS YEAR'S** date **DIVISIBLE BY 4?**

in years
by 4.

29

IF YOU ARE READING THIS ON FEBRUARY 29TH,

TODAY IS LEAP DAY

Tasmanian politician Sir James Wilson (1812–1880) was both **BORN AND DIED ON LEAP DAY.**

▶ What's the **FARTHEST** distance that **YOU CAN LEAP?**

53

MARCH

In 1997, scientists taught **TWO PIGS** to play a simple **VIDEO GAME.**

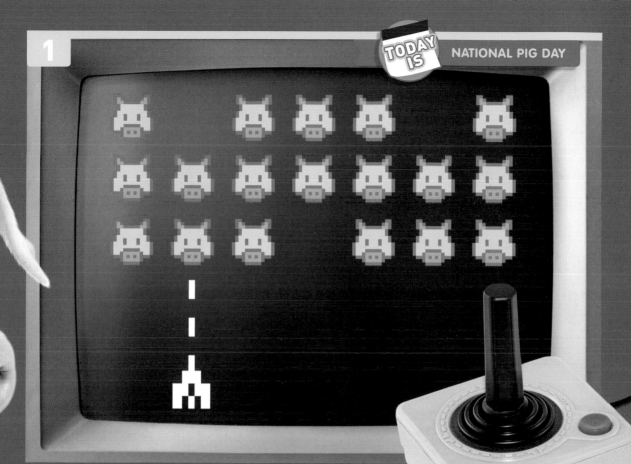

▶ Write **THREE MORE TRICKS** you think you could **TEACH A PIG** here.

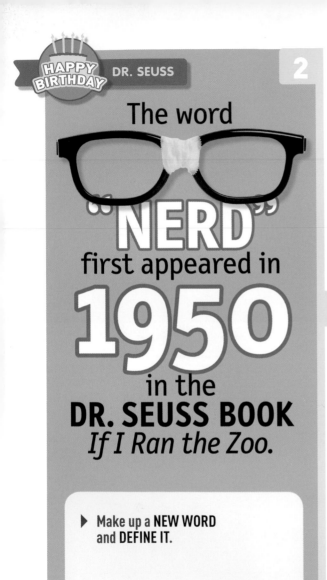

The word

"NERD"

first appeared in

1950

in the
DR. SEUSS BOOK
If I Ran the Zoo.

▶ Make up a **NEW WORD**
and **DEFINE IT.**

3

MAR

#1

In ancient Rome, calendars began with the month of March.

▶ If you could **REARRANGE THE MONTHS,**
what order would they go in?

4

MARCH IS SAID TO "COME IN LIKE A LION."

When **LIONS WALK,** their heels don't touch the ground.

▶ Write a **SILLY, SIX-LINE POEM** about **LIONS**.

"IKO IKO" and "OOH POO PAH DOO"
are popular songs sung during **MARDI GRAS.**

▶ What would you call your **MARDI GRAS SONG?**

5

6

POPSICLES
were invented by accident by an 11-year-old.

▶ **FREEZE A FOOD** you normally wouldn't, then **EAT IT.** Do you like it better **FROZEN OR UNFROZEN?**

TODAY IS NATIONAL FROZEN FOODS DAY

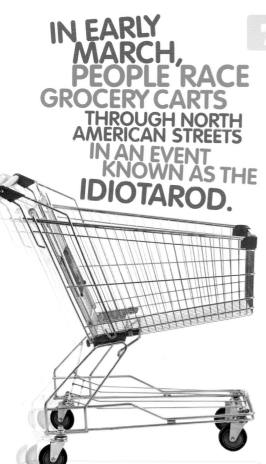

IN EARLY MARCH, PEOPLE RACE GROCERY CARTS THROUGH NORTH AMERICAN STREETS IN AN EVENT KNOWN AS THE **IDIOTAROD.**

▶ **QUIZ!** Which of the following is **NOT** a word that means a **STRANGE PERSON:**

A. oddball
B. beem
C. quiz

Answer: B

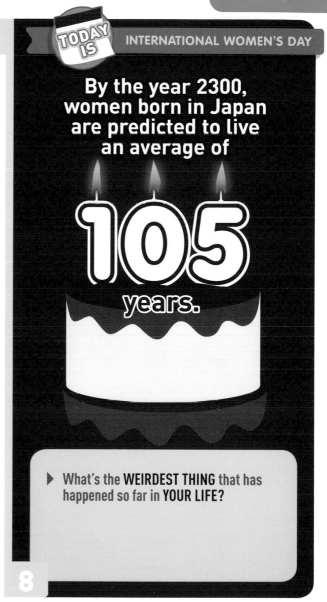

7

TODAY IS INTERNATIONAL WOMEN'S DAY

By the year 2300, women born in Japan are predicted to live an average of

105

years.

▶ What's the **WEIRDEST THING** that has happened so far in **YOUR LIFE?**

8

59

9

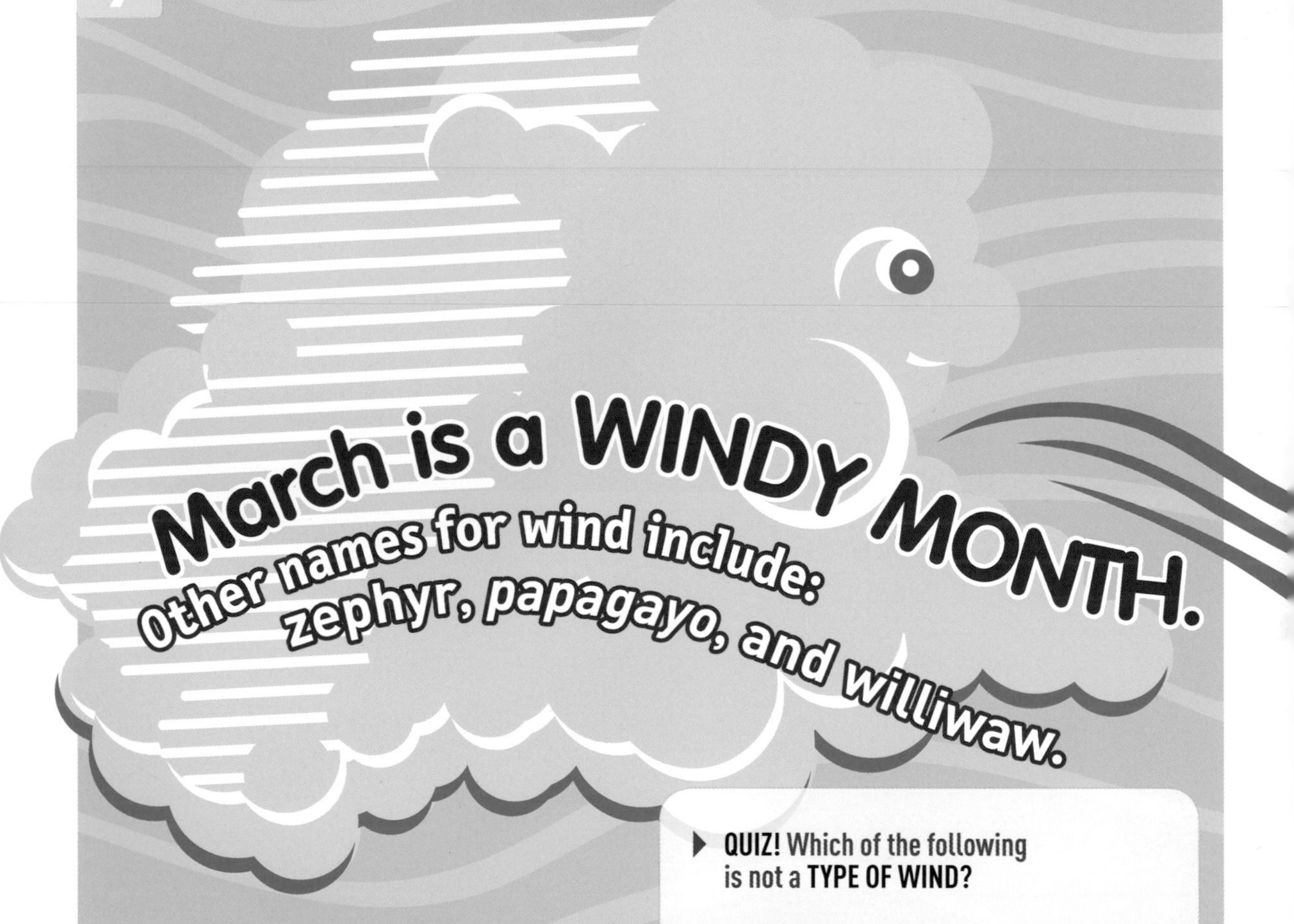

March is a WINDY MONTH.
Other names for wind include: zephyr, papagayo, and williwaw.

▶ **QUIZ!** Which of the following is not a **TYPE OF WIND?**

A. chinook
B. harmattan
C. booga-booga

Answer: C

10

At a March festival in Melbourne, Australia, people make **FLYING CONTRAPTIONS** and **JUMP OFF A PLATFORM** into a river to see **HOW FAR THEY CAN "FLY."**

▶ Draw a **FLYING CONTRAPTION** you would invent.

11
DAFFODILS AND TULIPS ARE poisonous to squirrels.

12
DURING THE 17TH-CENTURY Dutch tulip craze, PEOPLE WOULD PAY a year's salary FOR A SINGLE TULIP.

▶ **DRAW A PICTURE** of what you imagine the world's **MOST EXPENSIVE TULIP** would look like.

▶ What's the **WEIRDEST THING** you've ever seen a **SQUIRREL** do?

Each March at the Hindu Holi festival, people douse each other in brightly colored water and powder.

13

Wear as **MANY COLORS** as you can to school today. Place a photo of your outfit here.

14

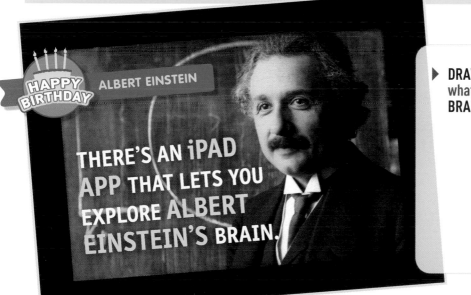

HAPPY BIRTHDAY

ALBERT EINSTEIN

THERE'S AN iPAD APP THAT LETS YOU EXPLORE ALBERT EINSTEIN'S BRAIN.

▶ **DRAW A PICTURE** of what you think your **BRAIN** looks like.

During
March Madness,

America's college
basketball championship
tournament, fans root for
teams whose mascots include
a gator, a badger,
... and a giant
fuzzy red blob.

▶ **PICK A MASCOT** to represent you and your
"team" of friends. **DRAW A PICTURE** of it
here, and **GIVE IT A NAME.**

16

Spring peepers, frogs known for their nighttime singing, can survive being **frozen for days.**

▶ Try to **DESCRIBE IN WORDS** the **WEIRDEST ANIMAL NOISE** you can think of.

17

 TODAY IS   ST. PATRICK'S DAY

LEPRECHAUNS
are rumored to live in the **WORLD'S SMALLEST CITY PARK**—roughly two feet (0.6 m) in diameter—in Portland, Oregon, U.S.A.

▶ What's the **WEIRDEST PLACE** in your hometown?

65

MARCH IS UMBRELLA MONTH.

▶ **MAKE AN UMBRELLA** using only things found in your closet. Place a photo of it here or sketch it.

WHEN IT RAINS,
ORANGUTANS
SOMETIMES MAKE
THEIR OWN UMBRELLAS
OUT OF LEAVES.

19 TODAY IS NATIONAL POULTRY DAY

In Gainesville, Georgia, U.S.A.—nicknamed the "chicken capital of the world"—it's illegal to eat fried chicken with a fork.

▶ **WRITE three new SILLY STATE LAWS.**

20

ON THE FIRST DAY OF SPRING, PEOPLE GATHER IN A NEW YORK CITY PARK TO TRY TO **balance eggs on one end** AT THE EXACT SAME SECOND.

▶ Try to **BALANCE AN EGG** on end. Record the number of tries it takes you.

21

THE MOON ISN'T **round.** IT'S EGG-SHAPED.

▶ **DRAW** a mini-map of the solar system below, but **CHANGE THE SHAPES** of all of the **PLANETS**.

22

"Spring chicken" IS SLANG FOR "a young person."

▶ Invent **SOME SLANG** for the words "spring," "chicken," and "egg."

▶ **DRAW A PICTURE** of what your face would look like if you **SMELLED A SKUNK.**

23

Skunk cabbage,
ONE OF THE FIRST PLANTS TO BLOOM IN SPRING, STINKS LIKE
rotten meat.

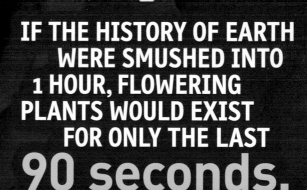

24

THE WORLD'S
biggest bloom
GROWS FROM AN
INDONESIAN PLANT
THAT HAS NO LEAVES OR ROOTS.

25

IF THE HISTORY OF EARTH
WERE SMUSHED INTO
1 HOUR, FLOWERING
PLANTS WOULD EXIST
FOR ONLY THE LAST
90 seconds.

The March March

march happens annually when students at the University of Cambridge, England, march from the town of March in the month of March.

▶ What's the **FARTHEST** you've ever **MARCHED**?

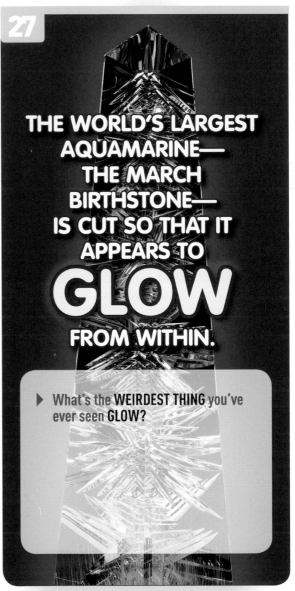

THE WORLD'S LARGEST AQUAMARINE— THE MARCH BIRTHSTONE— IS CUT SO THAT IT APPEARS TO GLOW FROM WITHIN.

▶ What's the **WEIRDEST THING** you've ever seen **GLOW**?

28

Ruby-throated hummingbirds,
which migrate to the U.S. in March, can't **walk** or **hop**—they can only fly or shuffle.

▶ If you **MIGRATED FOR THE WINTER,** where would you go?

29

▶ List three weird **THINGS YOU EAT.**

Rabbits excrete **PELLETS** of half-digested food called cecotropes. Then they **EAT THEM.**

73

March is said to "go out like a lamb." A male baby sheep is called a **RAM LAMB.**

▶ **QUIZ! Which of the following is NOT A NAME for a baby animal?**

A. porcupette
B. squeer
C. kid

Answer: B

31

It's **BROWN** now, but throughout history, the Eiffel Tower has been painted **RED, ORANGE,** and **YELLOW.**

▶ If you could paint a **FAMOUS LANDMARK** any color, which would **YOU CHOOSE** and what color would you paint it?

APRIL

In 1998, hungry customers lined up at Burger King to try the new **left-handed Whopper.**

TODAY IS APRIL FOOLS' DAY

▶ What's the best **APRIL FOOLS' PRANK** you've ever played on someone?

Surprise! It was an
April Fools' joke!

Ponce de León discovered Florida, U.S.A., on this day in 1513 while searching for the **Fountain of Youth.**

▶ Pretend you're an **EXPLORER** discovering **YOUR BACKYARD** for the first time. Record your observations below.

3

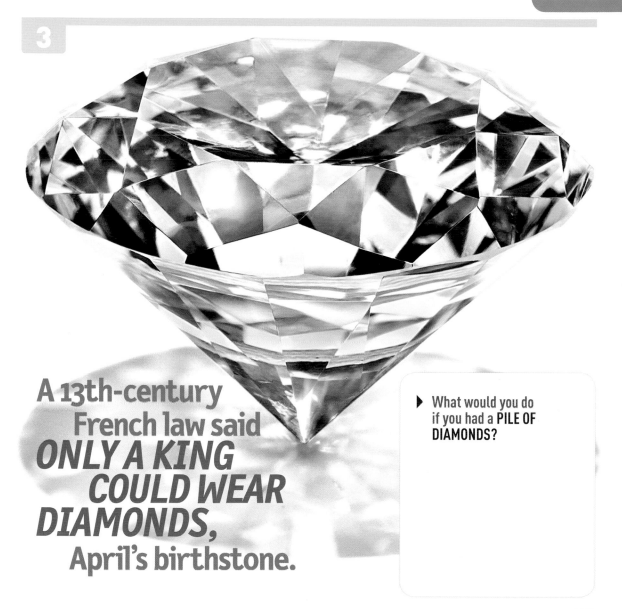

A 13th-century French law said **ONLY A KING COULD WEAR DIAMONDS**, April's birthstone.

▶ What would you do if you had a **PILE OF DIAMONDS?**

HAPPY BIRTHDAY MUDDY WATERS

Born MCKINLEY MORGANFIELD, blues guitarist MUDDY WATERS earned his nickname as a child because he liked to **PLAY IN THE MUD.**

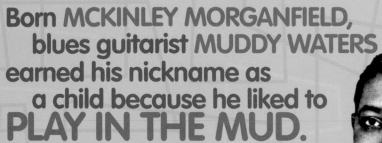

▶ Give yourself a **NEW NICKNAME** based on **WEIRD STUFF** you did as a little kid.

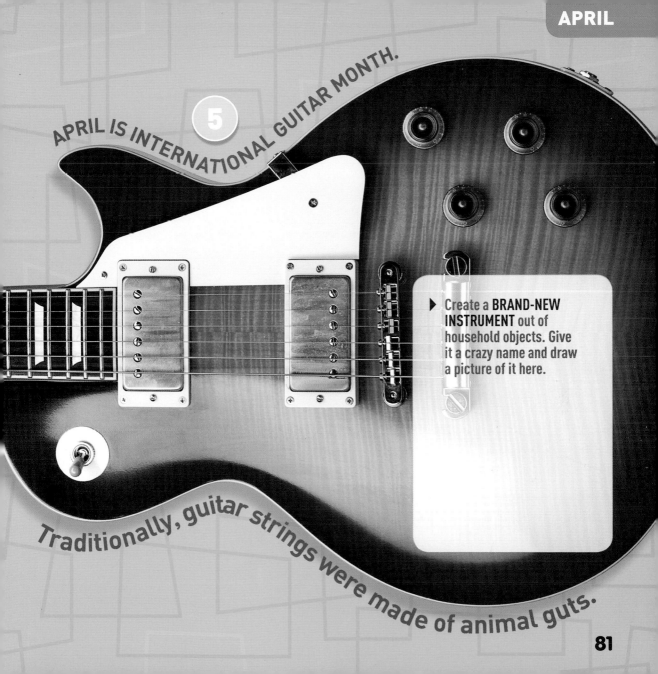

APRIL IS INTERNATIONAL GUITAR MONTH.

5

▶ Create a **BRAND-NEW INSTRUMENT** out of household objects. Give it a crazy name and draw a picture of it here.

Traditionally, guitar strings were made of animal guts.

81

AT THE NORTH POLE, FIRST REACHED BY EXPLORERS ON THIS DAY IN 1909, THE SUN RISES IN MARCH AND DOESN'T SET UNTIL SEPTEMBER.

▶ Have you ever tried to **STAY UP ALL NIGHT?** How did you pass the time?

7

In the middle of the 1800s, astronomer Jakob Lehmann calculated the date on which **Easter** will fall for the next **20,000 years.**

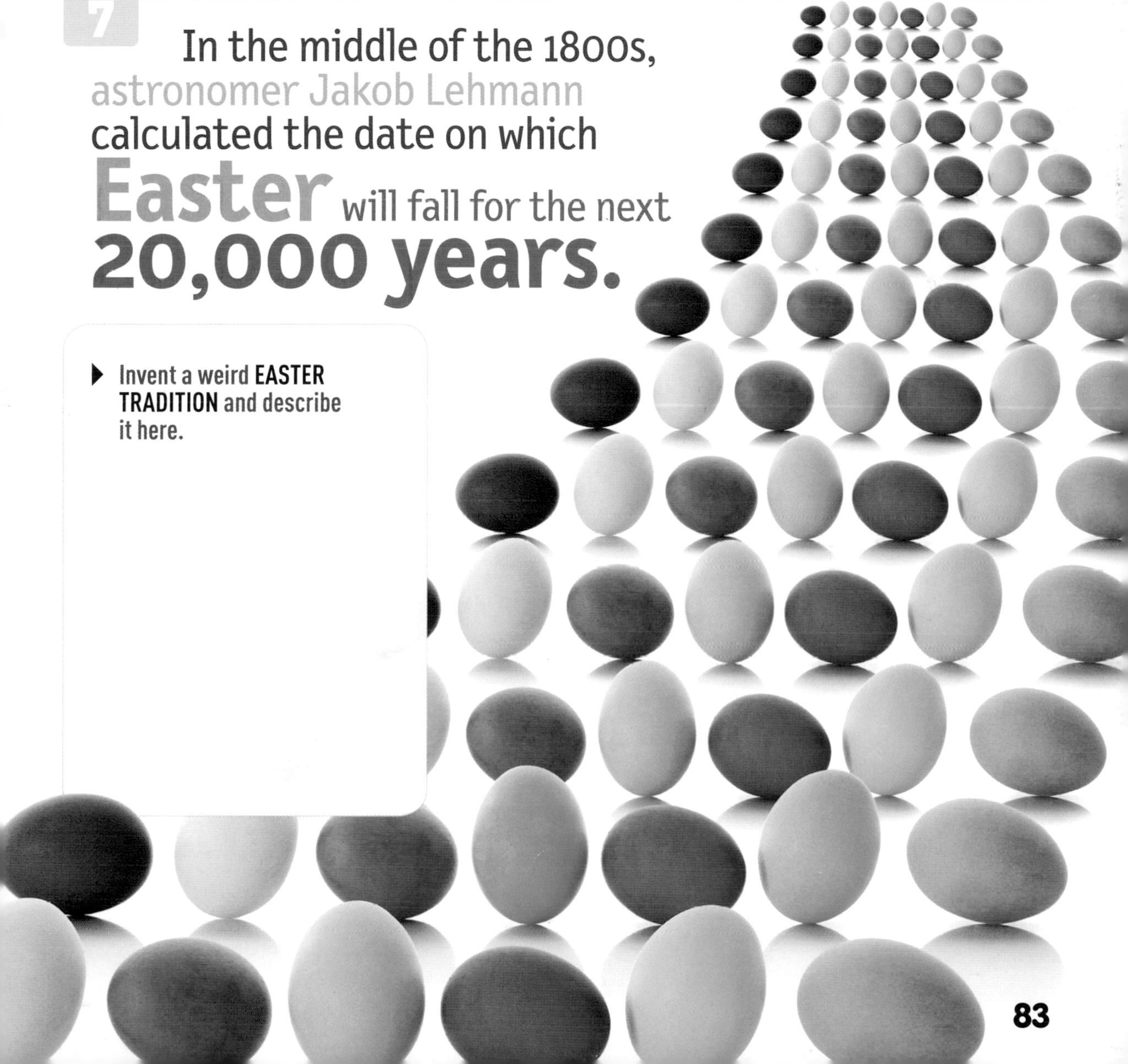

▶ Invent a weird **EASTER TRADITION** and describe it here.

Baby birds **learn to sing** when they are as young as **15 days old.**

▶ What was your FIRST WORD?

9

The first days of April and July always fall on the SAME DAY OF THE WEEK.

▶ **HOW MANY WORDS** can you make out of the words "APRIL" and "JULY"?

10

On baseball's Opening Day in April 1946, Boston Red Sox fans **SAT DOWN** to discover their seats were still coated in

WET PAINT.

▶ What's the **WEIRDEST THING** you've ever **SAT IN?**

Rabbits have nearly 360-DEGREE VISION, which means they can see IN ALMOST ALL DIRECTIONS at the same time.

▶ **BUNNIES IN YOUR NEIGHBORHOOD?** Keep a tally for one week and draw one bunny for every one you see in the space below.

12

Rabbits' teeth never STOP GROWING.

▶ **MEASURE YOUR TEETH.** How long are they?

During Thailand's
SONGKRAN FESTIVAL
each April, people
RIDE ELEPHANTS while
tossing buckets of
water on each other.

▶ Describe a time you were
unexpectedly **HIT WITH
WATER.**

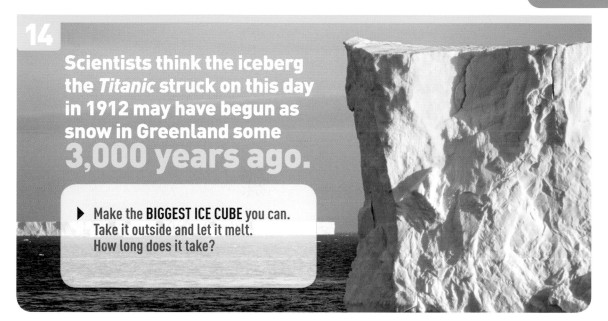

14

Scientists think the iceberg the *Titanic* struck on this day in 1912 may have begun as snow in Greenland some **3,000 years ago.**

▶ Make the **BIGGEST ICE CUBE** you can. Take it outside and let it melt. How long does it take?

15

*Roses are **red**.
Violets are **blue**.
April's National
Poetry Month. And
That's weird but true.*

▶ Write a **SILLY POEM** about your shoe.

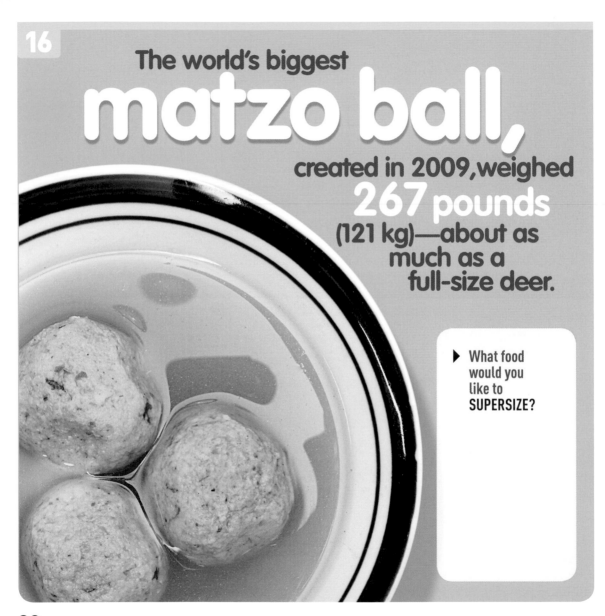

The world's biggest

matzo ball,

created in 2009, weighed **267 pounds** (121 kg)—about as much as a full-size deer.

▶ What food would you like to **SUPERSIZE?**

17

THE WORLD'S TINIEST BUTTERFLY HAS A

WINGSPAN SMALLER THAN A DIME.

▶ Hold your arms straight out at your sides. Measure from **FINGERTIP TO FINGERTIP.** How long is your **WINGSPAN?**

91

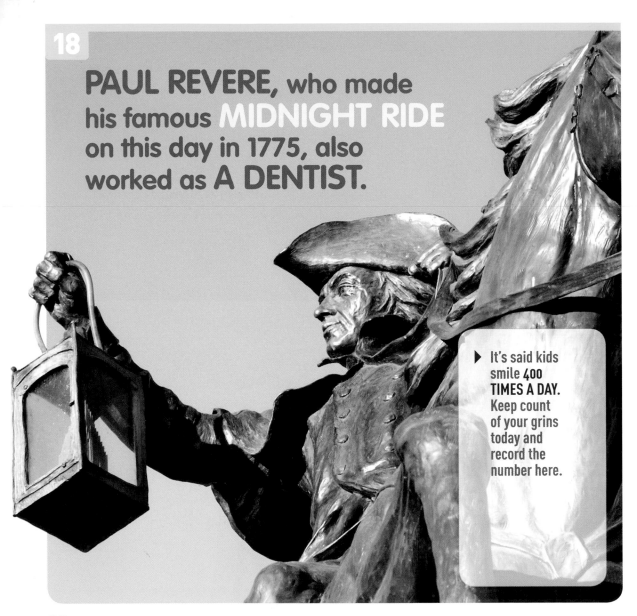

18

PAUL REVERE, who made his famous **MIDNIGHT RIDE** on this day in 1775, also worked as **A DENTIST.**

▶ It's said kids smile **400 TIMES A DAY.** Keep count of your grins today and record the number here.

19

SOME 1.4 MILLION PORTA-POTTIES ARE USED DURING THE BOSTON MARATHON, HELD ON THE THIRD MONDAY OF APRIL SINCE 1897.

TOILETS

▶ Describe your DREAM TOILET.

20

According to folklore, if there's **RAIN** on Easter morning, there'll be rain for the **NEXT SEVEN SUNDAYS.**

▶ Grab a bucket and place it outside to **CAPTURE RAINFALL.** How many inches did you get this week?

21

Egg-normous!

The largest Easter egg was over **25 feet** (7.6 m) high and weighed **8,968 pounds** (4,068 kg).

▶ What's the **WACKIEST** sort of **FILLING** you'd eat inside of an Easter egg?

22

Every year, candy-makers cook up some 16 million jelly beans!

▶ What **JELLY BEAN FLAVOR** would you invent?

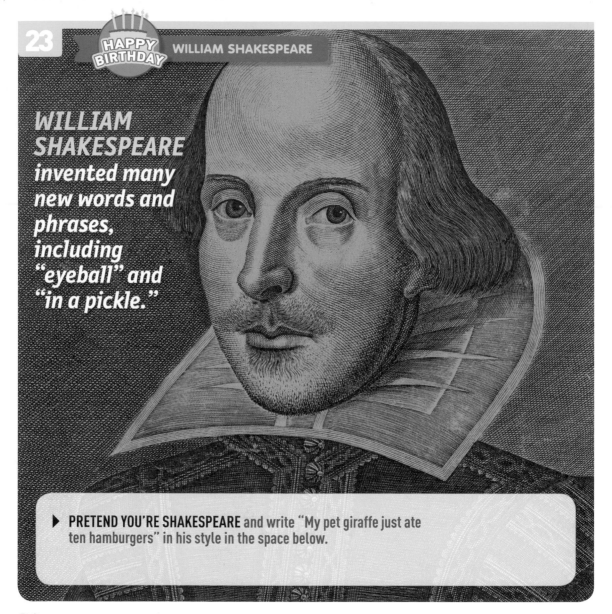

HAPPY BIRTHDAY WILLIAM SHAKESPEARE

WILLIAM SHAKESPEARE *invented many new words and phrases, including "eyeball" and "in a pickle."*

▶ **PRETEND YOU'RE SHAKESPEARE** and write "My pet giraffe just ate ten hamburgers" in his style in the space below.

24

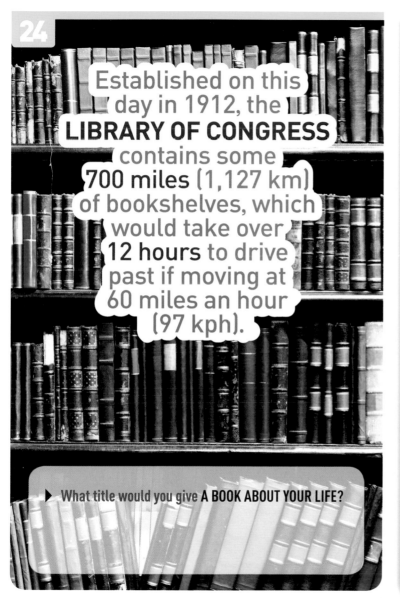

Established on this day in 1912, the **LIBRARY OF CONGRESS** contains some **700 miles (1,127 km)** of bookshelves, which would take over **12 hours** to drive past if moving at 60 miles an hour (97 kph).

▶ What title would you give **A BOOK ABOUT YOUR LIFE?**

25

KIDS GROW FASTEST IN THE SPRING.

▶ Are you **TALLER** in the morning or at night? Measure yourself twice today and record your results below.

Each April, folks in Laurel, Mississippi, U.S.A., compete to see how high they can blast **100-plus-pound** (45-kg) anvils into the sky.

▶ Which can you **THROW HIGHER:** a stuffed animal, a soccer ball, or a feather?

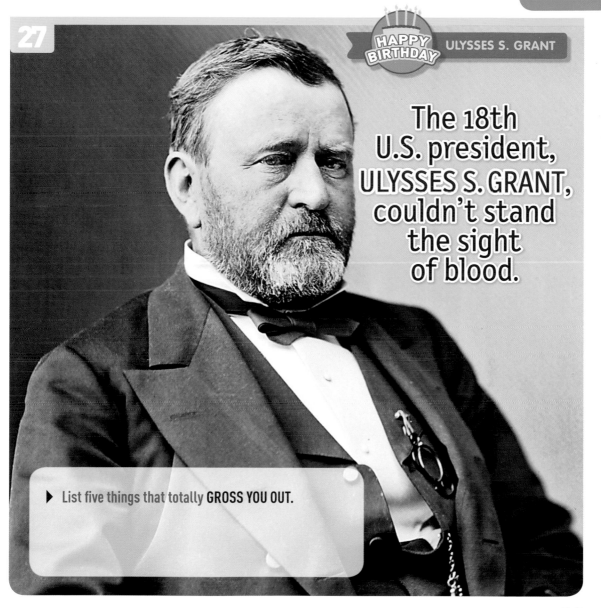

27

HAPPY BIRTHDAY
ULYSSES S. GRANT

The 18th U.S. president, **ULYSSES S. GRANT**, couldn't stand the sight of blood.

▶ List five things that totally **GROSS YOU OUT.**

28

DANDELIONS ARE USED AS A CURE FOR TUMMY TROUBLES IN TRADITIONAL CHINESE MEDICINE.

▸ Pluck a dandelion from outside and **PRESS IT** onto this page.

29

TODAY IS

NATIONAL ZIPPER DAY

The letters *YKK* found on most zippers stand for **Yoshida Kogyo Kabushikikaisha**—the world's largest zipper manufacturer.

▸ Take a look at **THE WRITING** on something you normally don't notice (the tag in your shirt or the underside of your cereal bowl for example). Write down what it says here.

30

April showers don't always bring May flowers. Too much April rain can make plants sick.

▶ What games do you like to **PLAY** in the **SPRING RAIN?**

MAY

The EMPIRE STATE BUILDING

—which opened on this day in 1931— is made of 10 MILLION BRICKS.

If you had 10 MILLION BRICKS, what would you build? Draw an outline of your building here.

May is named for MAIA, the Roman goddess of Spring.

If you could **RENAME** the month of May, what would you **CALL IT?**

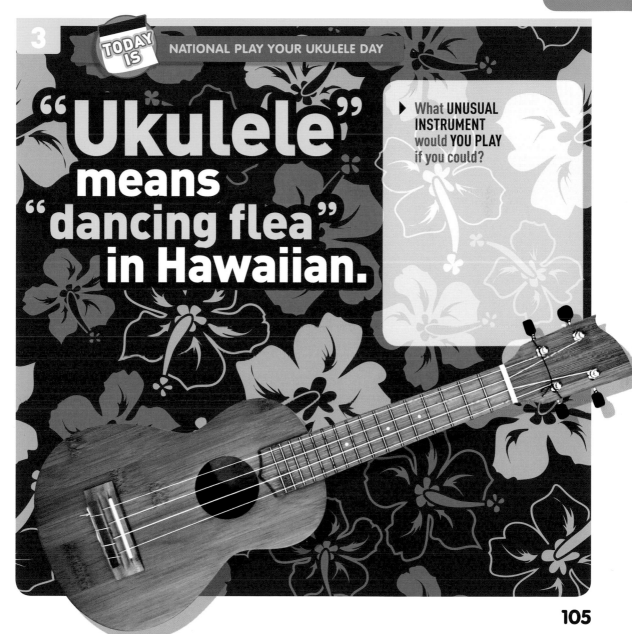

3

TODAY IS

NATIONAL PLAY YOUR UKULELE DAY

"Ukulele" means "dancing flea" in Hawaiian.

▶ What UNUSUAL INSTRUMENT would YOU PLAY if you could?

105

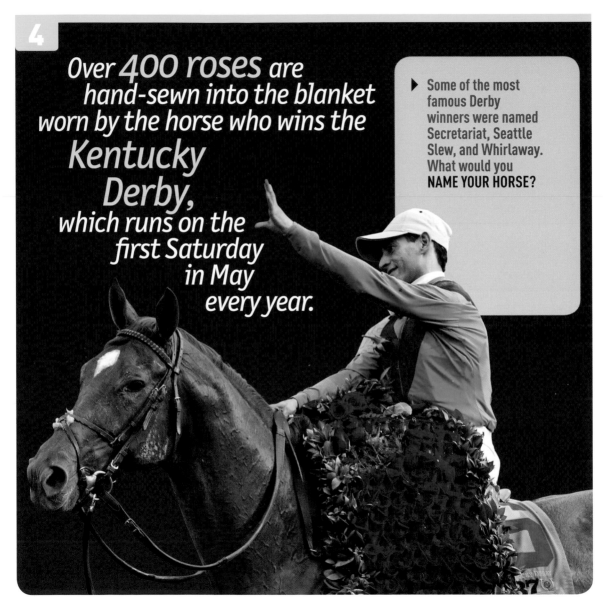

4

Over *400 roses* are hand-sewn into the blanket worn by the horse who wins the *Kentucky Derby,* which runs on the first Saturday in May every year.

▶ Some of the most famous Derby winners were named Secretariat, Seattle Slew, and Whirlaway. What would you **NAME YOUR HORSE?**

5

TODAY IS CINCO DE MAYO

The **Mexican** holiday CINCO DE MAYO is more popular in the **United States** than it is in **Mexico.**

▶ How do you **CELEBRATE** Cinco de Mayo?

6

In England, there's a museum with over

1,000 LAWN GNOMES.

▶ Create a **WACKY LAWN ORNAMENT** out of things you find around the house and put it in your **FRONT YARD**. List the materials you used here.

7

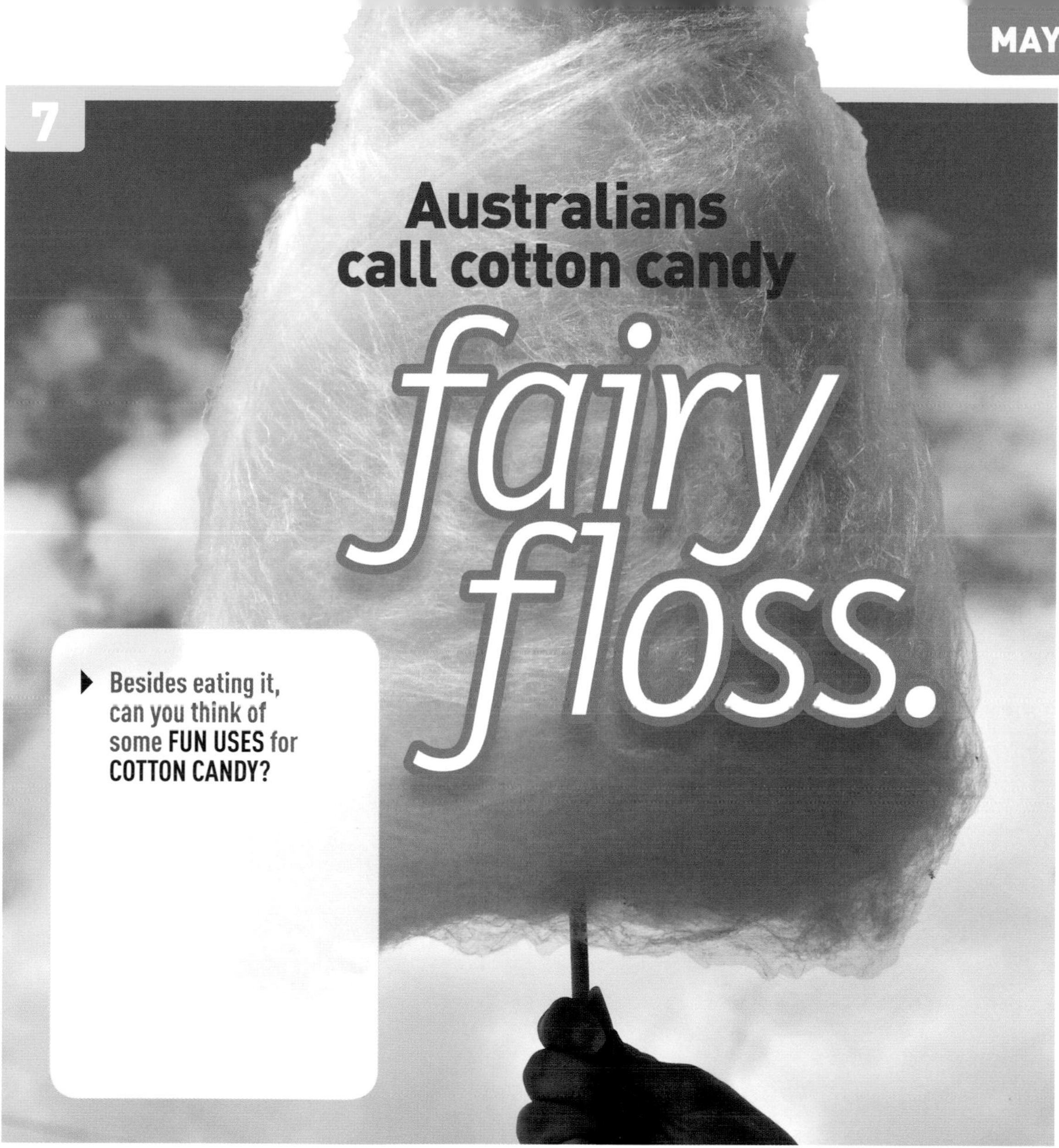

Australians call cotton candy *fairy floss.*

▶ Besides eating it, can you think of some **FUN USES** for **COTTON CANDY**?

Ancient Indians believed emeralds
—May's birthstone—
had magic healing properties.

▶ What **MAGICAL POWER** would you want most?

9

One thousand years ago, SOCKS were

▶ **HOW MANY** mismatched socks are in your drawer **RIGHT NOW?**

considered a sign of NOBILITY.

About **65%** of Mother's Day cards are purchased five days before the holiday.

Happy Mother's Day

▶ Write a four-line **MOTHER'S DAY POEM** here.

11

ANCIENT GREEKS
BELIEVED MINT

COULD CURE
HICCUPS.

▶ How do you
GET RID of your
HICCUPS?

WANTED

DOODLE DAY

Ronald Reagan WAS KNOWN FOR *doodling pictures* OF *cowboys.*

▶ **DOODLE** a picture of yourself **DOODLING.**

13

TODAY IS

FROG JUMPING DAY

▶ **LEAP LIKE A FROG** across your yard or down the sidewalk. How many jumps does it take to reach the end?

SOME **FROGS** CAN JUMP UP TO **20 TIMES** THEIR BODY LENGTH.

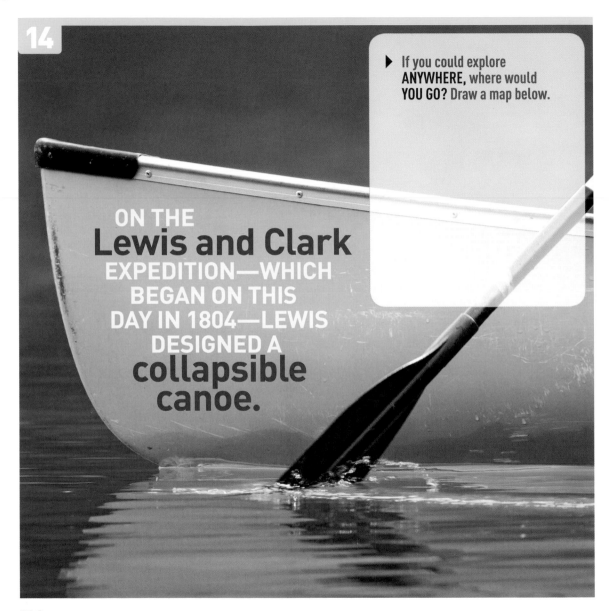

If you could explore **ANYWHERE,** where would **YOU GO?** Draw a map below.

ON THE
Lewis and Clark
EXPEDITION—WHICH BEGAN ON THIS DAY IN 1804—LEWIS DESIGNED A
collapsible canoe.

15

On this day in 1918,
the first airplane
carried mail
in the United States.

It was nicknamed
the "Jenny."

BY AIR MAIL
PAR AVION

▶ If you had **YOUR OWN AIRPLANE**, what would you call it?

MAY IS NATIONAL HAMBURGER MONTH.

▶ **WHAT EXTRAS** do you like on your hamburger? What extras do you **NOT LIKE** on your hamburger?

At the restaurant where hamburgers were invented, **KETCHUP** is strictly **FORBIDDEN.**

17

> If **YOUR CAT** was bad at catching mice, design a mousetrap that you'd use to **CATCH THEM.**

In English folklore, cats born in May are not good at catching mice.

President Harry S. Truman's middle name was "S."

(His parents couldn't decide on a full name.)

▶ Which U.S. president would you like to **PLAY VIDEO GAMES WITH?**

Harry S. Truman

USA 20c

▶ Invent a **WEIRD** Labor Day tradition to **CELEBRATE** in May.

Most countries celebrate LABOR DAY in May; the U.S. and Canada celebrate it in September.

20

Amelia Earhart

—WHO MADE THE FIRST FEMALE SOLO FLIGHT ACROSS THE ATLANTIC IN MAY 1932—HAD

imaginary friends

NAMED LAURA AND RINGA.

▶ **DO YOU** have an imaginary friend? Describe what he or she **LOOKS LIKE.** (If you don't have one, make one up!)

Can you think of **UNLUCKY THINGS** to do in May?

According to Cornish superstition, it is bad luck to buy a broom in May.

22

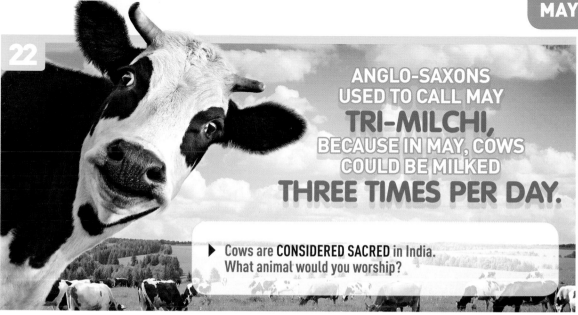

ANGLO-SAXONS
USED TO CALL MAY
TRI-MILCHI,
BECAUSE IN MAY, COWS
COULD BE MILKED
THREE TIMES PER DAY.

▶ Cows are **CONSIDERED SACRED** in India.
What animal would you worship?

23

May is International Respect for Chickens Month.
There are more chickens on Earth than people.

▶ Keep a tally of **HOW MANY PEOPLE** and **HOW MANY ANIMALS** you see today.
Which did you see more of?

24 **MORE PHOTOS** are taken in just two minutes today than were taken in the **ENTIRE 1800s.**

MAY IS NATIONAL PHOTO MONTH.

▶ Take a picture of something that **REPRESENTS YOUR LIFE** and place it here.

25 The **FIRST PHOTO** ever taken of a human was a man getting his **BOOTS SHINED.**

26 MEMORIAL DAY BECAME AN OFFICIAL HOLIDAY IN 1971.

▶ **INVENT A HOLIDAY** for your least favorite month.

27 During the construction of the Golden Gate Bridge, which opened on this day in 1937, builders strung **a net under the bridge to catch workers who fell.**

▶ Would you ever **BUNGEE-JUMP?**

28 The net saved **19 lives.**

▶ Name one time you were **SCARED OF HEIGHTS.**

30 A maypole built for Charles II was later used by **Isaac Newton** to hold his telescope.

29 Maypoles were once banned in England —anyone who erected one was fined **5 shillings per day.**

Did anything weird happen to you **THIS MONTH?**

31 No other month begins or ends on the same day of the week as May.

▶ If you **JUMBLE** up the letters of the word "May," **WHAT WORD** can you spell?

JUNE

The Atlantic Ocean's hurricane season officially begins today.

1

129

No hurricane's **name** ever begins with the letters Q, U, X, Y, or Z.

▶ **BREAK THE RULES!**
Make up hurricane names beginning with *Q, U, X, Y,* and *Z* and list them here.

2 Held in the late spring, England's Cotswold Olimpicks includes

WACKY SPORTING EVENTS

▶ Without looking up the rules, **IMAGINE THE WAYS** you could win a shin-kicking contest. Write them down here.

such as shin-kicking and tug-of-war.

③ TUG-OF-WAR

was once an **official event** in the **Summer Olympics.**

▶ QUIZ! Which of the following is **NOT** a former **OLYMPIC EVENT?**
A. water-skiing
B. arm wrestling
C. powerboating

Answer: B

131

4

JUNE BUGS

spend nine months underground before emerging during their

NAMESAKE MONTH.

▶ What would you do to pass the time if you had to **LIVE UNDERGROUND** for nine months?

5 "Coprolite" is a fancy word for **FOSSILIZED POOP.**

▶ Collecting coprolites is a popular pastime. List five other **WEIRD FOSSILIZED THINGS** you could **COLLECT.**

6 Dung beetles **DANCE** atop the balls of poop they push around.

▶ **MAKE UP A DANCE** a dung beetle might do and then perform it for someone. Draw a diagram of the moves here.

Yee-haw!

Mosquitoes ride raindrops to avoid being knocked off course by them while flying.

▶ Write a six-line
POEM ABOUT MOSQUITOES.

8

TODAY IS

WORLD OCEANS DAY

Dolphins name themselves.
Instead of a word, each animal responds to a specific high-pitched whistle.

▶ Come up with a **SOUND** that represents **YOU** and describe it here.

HAPPY BIRTHDAY DONALD DUCK

Donald Duck's middle name is Fauntleroy.

▶ Quack the "Happy Birthday" song in honor of Donald Duck's birthday. Do people recognize **WHAT YOU'RE SINGING?**

10

Every June in Portland, Oregon, U.S.A., thousands of people ride their bikes through the streets—

naked.

▶ What's the **SILLIEST** thing you've ever done **ON A BIKE?**

11

Every 13 or 17 years, millions of noisy **CICADAS** emerge from underground. Their collective buzzing can be **AS LOUD AS A MOTORCYCLE!**

▶ What's the **LOUDEST NOISE** you hear right now?

The Slip 'n Slide

was invented by a man after watching his son slide down their slick driveway.

▶ Come up with a **BACKYARD INVENTION** and describe it here.

▶ What's the biggest body of water you've ever gone **SWIMMING IN?**

About
20
Olympic-size
swimming pools could fit inside the world's largest swimming pool, in Algarrobo, Chile.

TODAY IS

NATIONAL SKUNK DAY

SKUNK SPRAY
can travel as far as
10 FEET! (3 m)

▶ If you could **SPRAY A STENCH,** what would you want it to smell like?

A TOMATO IS ALSO CALLED A **wolf peach** OR A **love apple.**

▶ **PICK A FRUIT** and come up with a **NICKNAME** for it. See if you can get it to catch on!

8 out of 10 LIVING THINGS on Earth are insects.

> ▶ Draw a picture of **YOURSELF** as some type of **INSECT.**

17 In late spring, **THOUSANDS OF FIREFLIES FLASH IN UNISON** each night for two weeks in Tennessee's **GREAT SMOKY MOUNTAINS NATIONAL PARK, U.S.A.**

▶ Using a flashlight, come up with a secret **BLINKING CODE** you can use to communicate with friends. What does **THREE FLASHES** mean?

18 TODAY IS INTERNATIONAL PICNIC DAY

FLIES, A COMMON PICNIC PEST, CAN'T EAT SOLID FOOD. INSTEAD THEY SPIT UP ON FOOD TO BREAK IT DOWN INTO **a liquid they can slurp up.**

▶ Eat like a fly: **MASH YOUR FOOD** until it's a **MUSHY MESS,** then slurp it up through a straw. Did it taste better?

143

19

▶ Walk around your house **LIKE A CHIMP.** Record the number of looks you receive here.

Even though chimpanzees are stronger than humans, people can throw a baseball five times faster.

20

▶ Imagine what it would be like if you lived on a planet where the **SUN NEVER SET.** In what weird ways would life be different?

AROUND THIS TIME EVERY YEAR,
20,000 PEOPLE
GATHER AT ENGLAND'S STONEHENGE FOR A
HUGE DANCE PARTY
TO CELEBRATE THE FIRST DAY OF SUMMER.

21

TODAY IS

GO SKATEBOARDING DAY

Tillman the ENGLISH BULLDOG once skateboarded 328 feet in just under 20 SECONDS.

▶ What animal do you think would be good at **RIDING A SKATEBOARD**? Why?

Dogs SWEAT only through their PAWS.

▶ What's the **WEIRDEST PLACE** on your body that sweats?

23

YOUR SWEAT

CONTAINS MANY OF THE SAME SUBSTANCES AS YOUR PEE.

▶ Write a **FUNNY RHYME** about sweat here.

24

When you eat   you're actually eating teeny-tiny **ROCKS.**

▶ List three other things from nature that **YOU EAT.**

147

▶ Describe another weird way you could **CATCH A FISH.**

Held in Oklahoma, U.S.A., every June, the Okie Noodling Tournament sees who can catch the biggest catfish,

USING THEIR BARE HANDS!

26

Fish called Asian carp have broken people's bones by suddenly *flinging themselves* out of the water and into boats.

▶ What's the weirdest thing you've ever seen **JUMP OUT** of the water?

27

Slender glass lizards have no legs and look JUST LIKE SNAKES.

▶ Draw a picture of a **BIRD** that **LOOKS** like a fish.

▶ Write down as many **MISLEADING** animal names that you can think of.

28

Horned toads aren't toads at all— THEY'RE LIZARDS.

Fingernails, on average, grow as fast as Earth's tectonic plates move — ABOUT AN INCH A YEAR.

(2.5 cm)

▶ Collect a sample FINGERNAIL clipping and TAPE IT HERE.

30

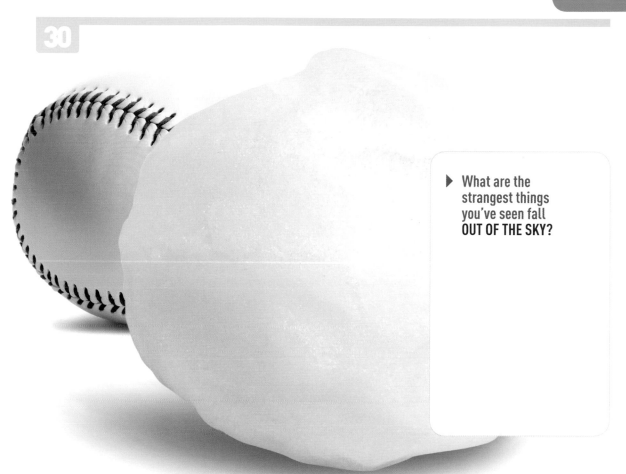

> What are the strangest things you've seen fall **OUT OF THE SKY?**

BASEBALL-SIZE HAILSTONES FELL ON BOZEMAN, MONTANA, U.S.A., ON THIS DAY IN 2010.
THEY HAD TINY BACTERIA LIVING INSIDE THEM.

JULY

1

Some cyclists who rode in the first **Tour de France,** on this day in 1903, cheated by hopping on trains and riding in cars.

▸ Design a **WEIRD RACE** through your neighborhood. Describe it here.

155

JULY IS NATIONAL BLUEBERRY MONTH.

Early American colonists made gray paint by boiling blueberries in milk.

▶ What items around your home could you use to **MAKE PAINT?**

3 One out of four Americans doesn't know that the U.S. **DEFEATED GREAT BRITAIN** during the Revolutionary War.

▶ **QUIZ!** Which of these birds is the one that Founding Father **BEN FRANKLIN** wanted to be the **U.S. NATIONAL BIRD?**
A. bald eagle
B. cardinal
C. blue jay
D. turkey

Answer: D

TODAY IS   INDEPENDENCE DAY

▶ What's something weird you would eat **ON YOUR HOT DOG?**

4 Americans eat **155 MILLION** hot dogs every **FOURTH OF JULY.**

During Sonkajärvi, Finland's annual Wife-Carrying Festival, husbands compete to see who can carry their wife through an obstacle course the fastest.

▸ How far can you **CARRY** someone **PIGGYBACK?**

6

Philadelphia's **CRACKED** Liberty Bell hasn't been rung *SINCE 1846.*

▶ What objects symbolize **LIBERTY** to you? Draw three of them here.

> What **COLORFUL NAMES** would you give your best **ATHLETIC MOVES**? Describe each maneuver and sport.

7 IN THE 1930s, BASEBALL GREAT SATCHEL PAIGE

named his pitches

the Hesitation, the Submariner, and the Bat Dodger.

8 PLAYED IN 1981, the longest professional baseball game lasted

8 hours 25 minutes.

> What's the **LONGEST SPORTING EVENT** you've ever played in? How long did it last?

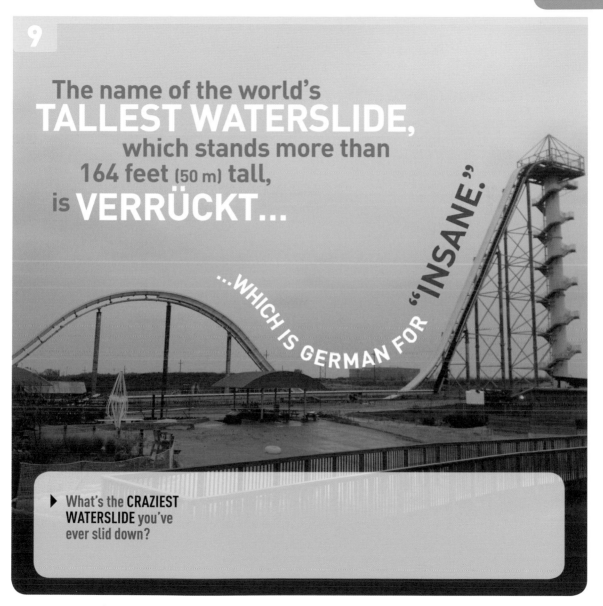

9

The name of the world's
TALLEST WATERSLIDE,
which stands more than
164 feet (50 m) **tall,**
is **VERRÜCKT...**

...WHICH IS GERMAN FOR "INSANE."

▶ What's the **CRAZIEST WATERSLIDE** you've ever slid down?

10

HAPPY BIRTHDAY **NIKOLA TESLA**

Nikola Tesla,

nicknamed the "father of the electrical age," was

born during a lightning storm.

▶ What was the **WEATHER** like on the day **YOU WERE BORN?** (Hint: Ask your parents.)

11

TODAY IS **WORLD POPULATION DAY**

In 2011, the world population reached

7 BILLION.

Seven billion steps would take you around the globe

133 TIMES.

▶ Count the number of **STEPS YOU TAKE** today and write it here.

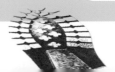

TODAY IS

NATIONAL COW APPRECIATION DAY **12**

No two black-and-white Holstein cows have the exact same spots.

▶ **HOW MANY** foods can you think of that **COME FROM COWS?**

13 ## July is National Ice Cream Month.
The average American eats 5½ gallons (21 L) of ice cream each year.

▶ If you could have only **ONE FLAVOR** of ice cream for the **REST OF YOUR LIFE**, what would it be?

163

14

TODAY IS

BASTILLE DAY

The **BASTILLE PRISON,** which was stormed on this day in 1789 during the French Revolution, held only seven prisoners at the time.

▶ **QUIZ!** Which one of these food names is **NOT** French?
A. french fries
B. soufflé
C. crepe
D. omelette

Answer: A

15

IN FRANCE, IT IS ILLEGAL TO
NAME YOUR PIG
NAPOLEON.

▶ What would you name a PET PIG?

16

Lemons

have been used since ancient times as an insecticide, cleaner, and medicine.

▶ Set up a **LEMONADE STAND** with your friends. Take a picture of your business and paste it here.

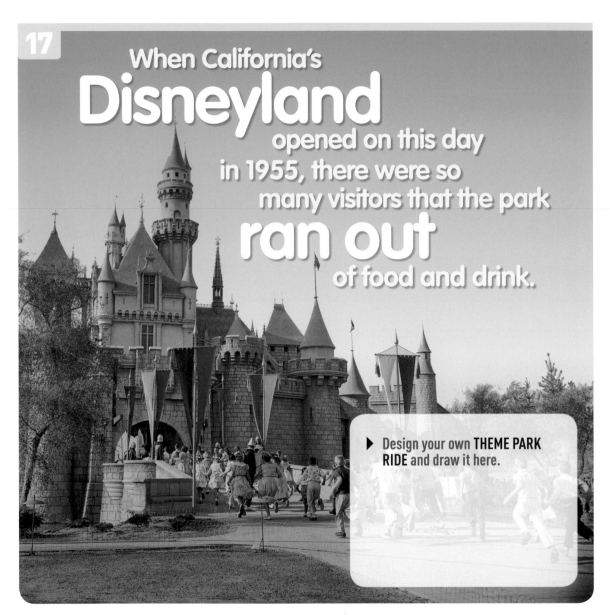

When California's
Disneyland
opened on this day
in 1955, there were so
many visitors that the park
ran out
of food and drink.

▶ Design your own **THEME PARK RIDE** and draw it here.

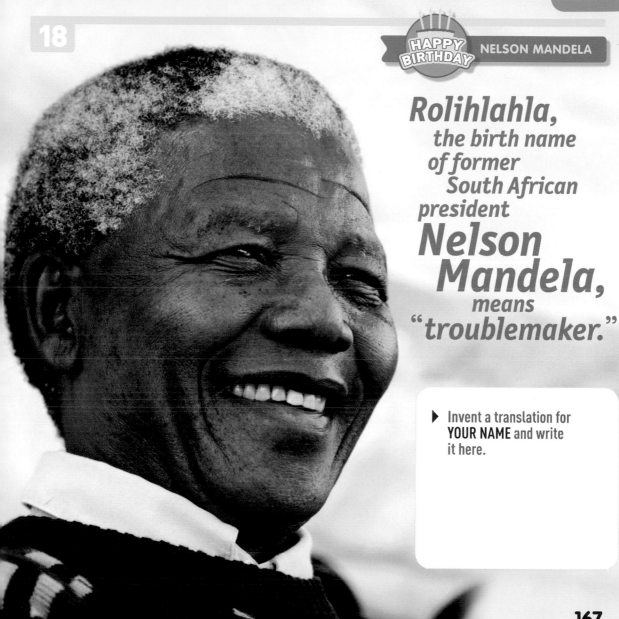

18

HAPPY BIRTHDAY NELSON MANDELA

Rolihlahla,
the birth name
of former
South African
president
Nelson
Mandela,
means
"troublemaker."

▶ Invent a translation for
YOUR NAME and write
it here.

▶ The Rosetta Stone helped scientists **TRANSLATE** ancient Egyptian **HIEROGLYPHICS**. Create your own **SECRET ALPHABET** made of pictures.

THE Rosetta Stone, DISCOVERED ON THIS DAY IN 1799, HAS BEEN ON DISPLAY IN THE BRITISH MUSEUM IN LONDON FOR MORE THAN 200 years.

20

If you could **TRAVEL** to **ANY PLANET** or moon, which one would you choose?

On this day in 1969, **ASTRONAUT BUZZ ALDRIN** became the first person to **PEE ON THE MOON**, through a tube fitted into his space suit.

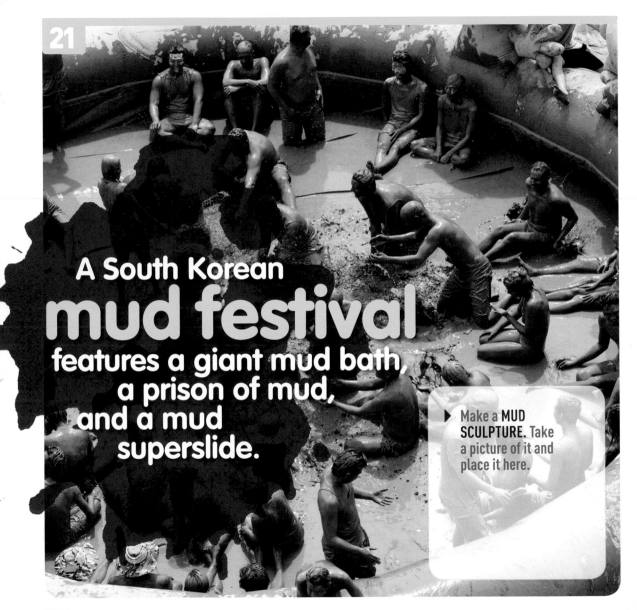

A South Korean

mud festival

features a giant mud bath,
a prison of mud,
and a mud
superslide.

▶ Make a MUD
SCULPTURE. Take
a picture of it and
place it here.

22

TODAY IS — HAMMOCK DAY

HAMMOCKS were invented so people could sleep off the ground, avoiding **VENOMOUS BUGS AND SNAKES!**

▶ What would be your **DREAM BED?**

23

AUGIE, A GOLDEN RETRIEVER, CAN HOLD A RECORD **FIVE** TENNIS BALLS IN HER MOUTH **AT ONCE!**

▶ How long does it take you to pick up an **APPLE** using only your teeth?

171

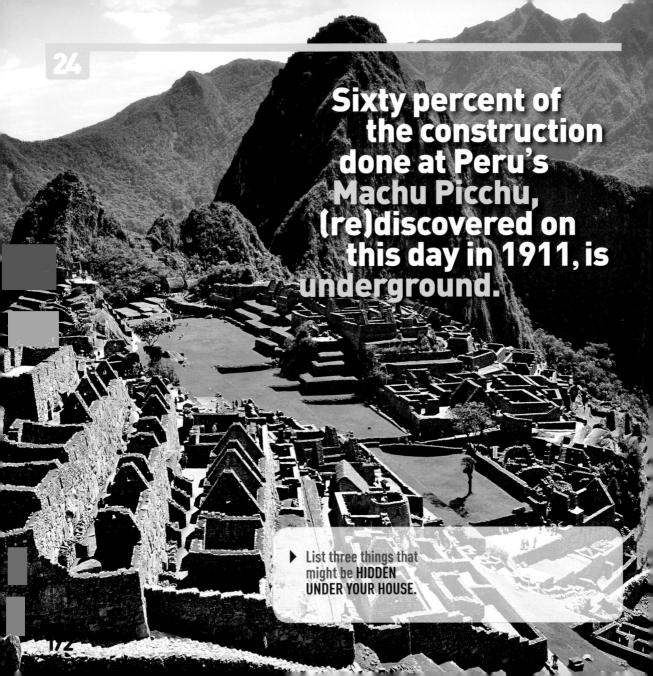

Sixty percent of the construction done at Peru's Machu Picchu, (re)discovered on this day in 1911, is underground.

▶ List three things that might be **HIDDEN UNDER YOUR HOUSE.**

25

The first sunglasses, invented in 12TH-CENTURY CHINA, were made of slabs of quartz.

▶ **DRAW** what you think that very first pair of shades might have **LOOKED LIKE.**

26

TODAY IS   NATIONAL DAY OF THE COWBOY

10 FEET (3 m) TALL AND 44 FEET (13 m) WIDE, *the world's biggest cowboy hat* CAN BE FOUND IN SEATTLE, WASHINGTON, U.S.A.

▶ Write down all the **COWBOY WORDS** you can think of here.

AT CALIFORNIA'S GILROY
GARLIC FESTIVAL,
TREATS INCLUDE GARLIC FRENCH FRIES, GARLIC POPCORN, AND
GARLIC ICE CREAM.

▶ **QUIZ!** Garlic is related to a lot of plants, but **WHICH ONE** of these is **NOT** in the family?
A. leek
B. scallion
C. chive
D. turnip

Answer: D

28

TODAY IS

NATIONAL MILK CHOCOLATE DAY

MELTED CHOCOLATE
in someone's pocket inspired the invention of the **MICROWAVE.**

▶ What's your **FAVORITE KIND** of chocolate?

On this day in 1981, Prince Charles married Lady Diana Spencer while **750 million people watched** *(on live TV)*.

▶ **HOW MANY** people could fit in your living room at the **SAME TIME?**

30

PLUSH TOYS ride astride **SHEEP** at the annual Sheep Racing Festival held on the U.K.'s Isle of Sark in late July.

▶ Which stuffed animal would you pick **TO RIDE A SHEEP?**

31

The world's largest Popsicle-stick sculpture contains 840,000 sticks and depicts a giant map of Thailand.

▶ Create the **LARGEST** Popsicle-stick structure you can. How many sticks did you use?

177

AUGUST

1

THE FIRST SIX FLAGS AMUSEMENT PARK OPENED ON THIS DAY IN 1961.

The name **Six Flags** refers to the flags of six nations that governed Texas throughout its history: SPAIN, FRANCE, MEXICO, REPUBLIC OF TEXAS, CONFEDERATE STATES OF AMERICA, AND UNITED STATES OF AMERICA.

▶ Pretend you **GOVERN A COUNTRY.** Give it a name and draw its flag here.

2

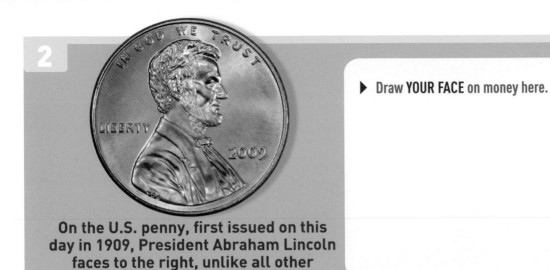

On the U.S. penny, first issued on this day in 1909, President Abraham Lincoln faces to the right, unlike all other presidents on coins, who face left.

▶ Draw **YOUR FACE** on money here.

3

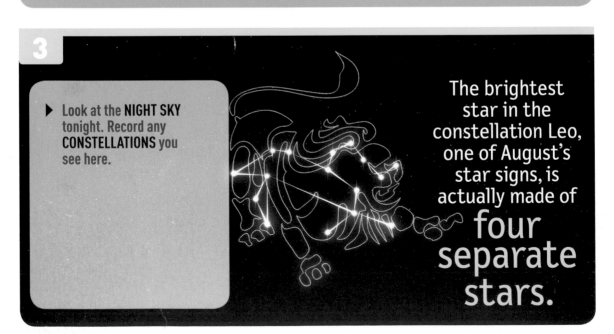

▶ Look at the **NIGHT SKY** tonight. Record any **CONSTELLATIONS** you see here.

The brightest star in the constellation Leo, one of August's star signs, is actually made of **four separate stars.**

4

HAPPY BIRTHDAY BARACK OBAMA

▶ Take a poll: Ask your friends if they could have **ANY PET** they wanted, what would it be? Which animal comes in first?

Growing up, President Barack Obama had a **PET APE** named Tata.

5

> **QUIZ!** Which one of these U.S. presidents was **NOT A REDHEAD?**
> A. Thomas Jefferson
> B. Dwight D. Eisenhower
> C. Andrew Jackson
> D. Woodrow Wilson

Answer: D

THE "LITTLE ORPHAN ANNIE" COMIC STRIP, WHICH DEBUTED ON THIS DAY IN 1924, STARRED A LITTLE RED-HAIRED GIRL.

REDHEADS MAKE UP
LESS THAN ONE PERCENT
OF THE WORLD'S POPULATION.

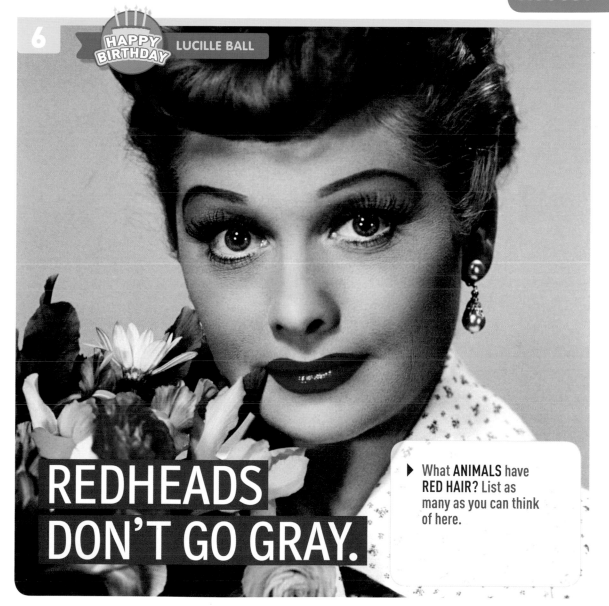

6

HAPPY BIRTHDAY LUCILLE BALL

REDHEADS DON'T GO GRAY.

▶ What **ANIMALS** have **RED HAIR**? List as many as you can think of here.

183

▶ If you had to cross the Pacific Ocean **ON A RAFT,** what kind would you build? What materials would you use?

On this day in 1947, Thor Heyerdahl completed his 101-day trip across the Pacific Ocean on a **40-SQUARE-FOOT RAFT.** (4 m²)

8

France's Pourcailhade, held the second Sunday of August, celebrates

ALL THINGS PIG

with piglet races, people pig-squealing contests, and all the pork you can eat!

▶ Have a family competition to see who can mimic the best **PIG SQUEAL**. Whom did you name the winner?

▶ What's the coolest thing you've ever **BUILT AT THE BEACH?**

THE WORLD'S TALLEST SAND CASTLE, constructed in 2013 in Point Pleasant, New Jersey, U.S.A., was taller than a three-story building.

9

185

NATIONAL S'MORES DAY

S'mores
were originally called "Some Mores."

▸ What's your **DREAM S'MORE?**
Draw a diagram of it here.

11

▶ Build a 'MALLOW CASTLE using a whole bag of marshmallows. How tall is your structure?

Americans buy
90 MILLION POUNDS (40,823,300 kg)
of marshmallows each year.

12 Surfing was invented by ancient Polynesians in Hawaii, which became a U.S. territory on this day in 1898.

▶ Create your own SURFBOARD DESIGN.

13 Astronauts lived for four months inside Hawaii's Mauna Loa volcano to simulate life on Mars.

> If you were to travel to MARS, what five things would you bring?

14 The volcanic gem peridot, August's birthstone, symbolizes the tears of Pele, the Hawaiian goddess of fire and volcanoes.

> If you could RENAME a volcano, what name would you choose?

189

> ▶ What **STRANGE NOISES** do you hear at night? Do you know what causes them?

Some sand dunes make

mysterious sounds

like whistling, singing, barking, or even the croaking of a frog.

16

▶ What's the weirdest thing you've ever seen at a **YARD SALE?**

The world's longest
YARD SALE
—held each August along Highway 127— stretches **690 miles** (1,110 km) from Michigan to Alabama, U.S.A.

17

The crew of the *Double Eagle II*, which completed the first
TRANSATLANTIC BALLOON FLIGHT
on this day in 1978, survived on sardines and hot dogs.

▶ If you could **EAT ONE FOOD** for a month, what would you choose?

191

Every August, Finland hosts the **Air Guitar World Championships.**

▶ Have an **AIR GUITAR CONTEST** with your friends. Put a bunch of song names in a hat, and have each person pick one at random to perform. What was the crowd favorite?

19

▶ What **OTHER OBJECTS** could be used as Frisbees?

In the 1920s, college students invented the first Frisbees by playing catch with empty pie tins.

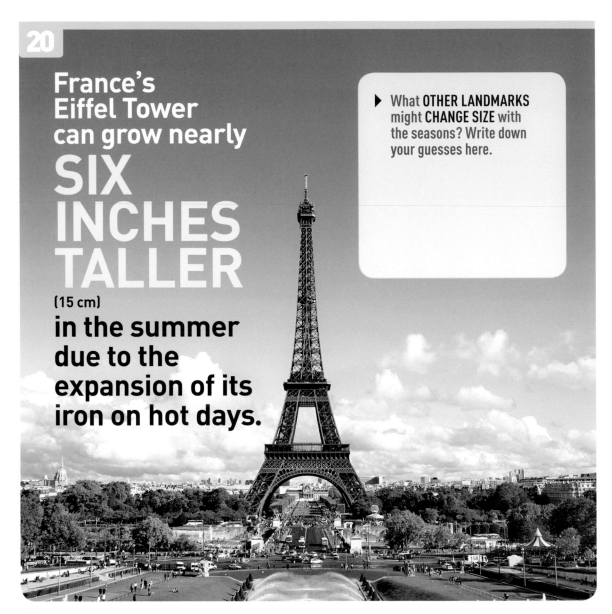

20

France's
Eiffel Tower
can grow nearly

SIX INCHES TALLER

(15 cm)

in the summer
due to the
expansion of its
iron on hot days.

▶ What **OTHER LANDMARKS** might **CHANGE SIZE** with the seasons? Write down your guesses here.

21 Only *female* mosquitoes can suck blood.

▶ What weird ways can you think of to **KEEP MOSQUITOES AWAY** from your summer fun?

22 Mosquitoes use *body odor to find victims.*

▶ If you could **BE ANY INSECT,** which would you choose and why?

On this day in 1784, four counties in western North Carolina declared independence from the United States and named their "nation"

Franklin.

▶ In this space, draw a **FLAG** for your own **NEW NATION.**

24

POTATO PARTY!

Events at Barenville, Minnesota, U.S.A.'s Potato Days festival include potato picking, potato carving, and mashed-potato wrestling.

▶ What's **YOUR FAVORITE WAY** to eat a potato?

25

Participants in Derbyshire, England's

Toe Wrestling Championships

place their toes on the "toedium" and go at it.

▶ Host a **TOE WRESTLING** tournament with **YOUR FRIENDS.** Who has the strongest toes?

197

Events at Wales's *World Alternative Games* include office-chair racing, gravy wrestling, bog snorkeling, and worm charming.

▶ **WORM CHARMERS** compete to see how many worms they can get out of the ground without digging. How would you charm earthworms out of the dirt?

27 Early **explorers used** watermelons as **canteens.**

▶ What other objects can be made out of watermelons? Draw your **WATERMELON INVENTIONS** here.

28

A watermelon is 92 percent water.

▶ How many different ways can you think of to **EAT WATERMELON?** List them here.

29

At Valencia, Spain's La Tomatina festival, thousands of people toss **squashed tomatoes** at each other.

▶ What's the **FARTHEST** you can **TOSS** a tomato?

30

HAPPY BIRTHDAY   MARY SHELLEY

MARY SHELLEY WROTE THE SCARY NOVEL

FRANKENSTEIN,

WHOSE MONSTER HAS APPEARED TWICE ON U.S. POSTAGE STAMPS.

▶ List your **TOP FIVE SCARIEST** monsters here.

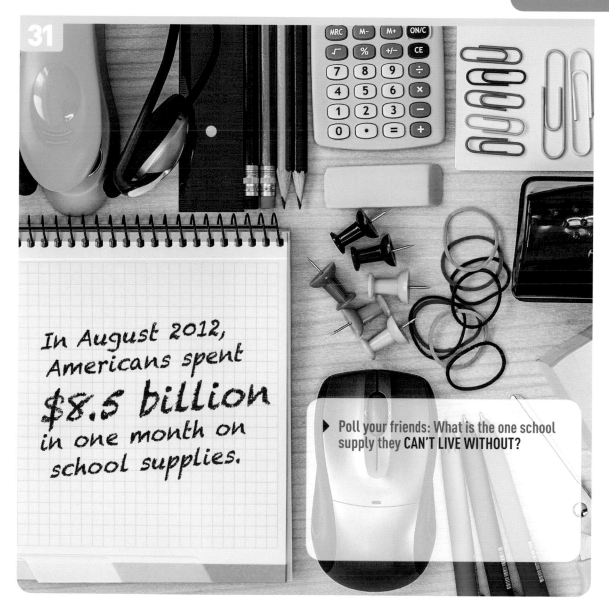

31

In August 2012, Americans spent **$8.5 billion** in one month on school supplies.

Poll your friends: What is the one school supply they **CAN'T LIVE WITHOUT?**

SEPTEMBER

CHESS PRODIGY BOBBY FISCHER WON THE INTERNATIONAL CHESS CROWN ON THIS DAY IN 1972.

1

IN CHESS, THERE ARE
318,979,564,000
WAYS TO PLAY THE FIRST
FOUR MOVES OF THE GAME.

▶ Pick out a game you love. How many possible **FIRST MOVES** are there? 1 to 10? 11 to 50? 51 to 100? Too many to count?

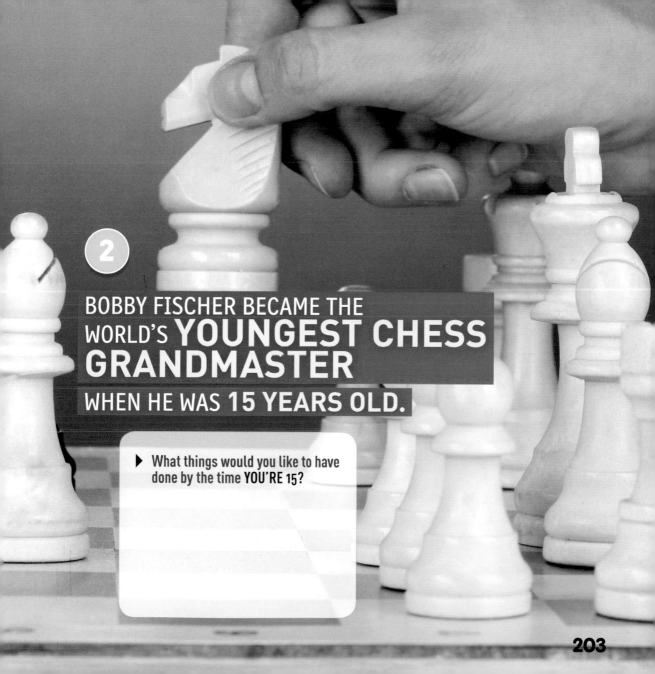

2

BOBBY FISCHER BECAME THE WORLD'S **YOUNGEST CHESS GRANDMASTER** WHEN HE WAS **15 YEARS OLD.**

▶ What things would you like to have done by the time **YOU'RE 15?**

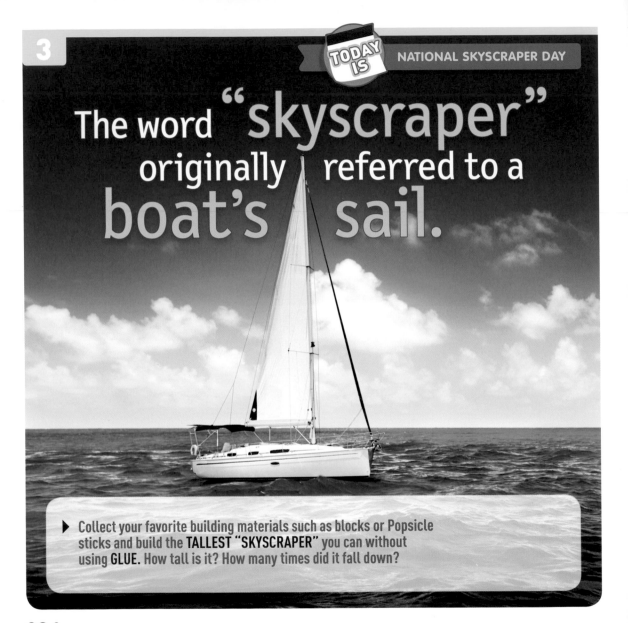

The word "skyscraper" originally referred to a boat's sail.

▶ Collect your favorite building materials such as blocks or Popsicle sticks and build the **TALLEST "SKYSCRAPER"** you can without using **GLUE.** How tall is it? How many times did it fall down?

4

Most of the world's vines grow in a counterclockwise direction, except for

MORNING GLORIES,

September's birth flower, which wrap clockwise.

▶ Go outside and draw a picture of the **FIRST FLOWER** you see.

5

The world record for the
biggest pig
was set in 1933 by Big Bill,
who weighed
2,552 pounds (1,157 kg),
stood **5 feet** (1.5 m) tall,
and measured **9 feet** (2.7 m) long.

▶ What's the **BIGGEST ANIMAL** you've ever seen in person? Draw a picture of it here.

6

The weirdly named
Piggly Wiggly,
the first modern grocery store, opened on
this day in 1916 in Memphis, Tennessee, U.S.A.

▶ Choose an adjective (stinky, slimy, jiggly, smelly, etc.) and an animal to come up with a **NEW GROCERY STORE NAME.**

HAPPY BIRTHDAY GRANDMA MOSES

GRANDMA MOSES,

one of America's most famous painters, didn't begin painting until she was in her 70s!

▶ When you're in your 70s, what kinds of **NEW HOBBIES** will you try? Write them down here.

TODAY IS GRANDPARENTS DAY

A PENNSYLVANIA MAN

had 11 kids, 97 grandkids, 634 great-grandkids, and 82 great-great-grandkids.

▶ **HOW MANY GRANDKIDS** are there in your family?

9

California,
which became a U.S. state on this date in 1850, is likely named after Calafia, a mythical **warrior queen.**

▶ **HOW MANY SONGS** can you think of **ABOUT CALIFORNIA** or places in California? Write them down here.

PINK and ORANGE SAPPHIRES,

September's birthstone, can cost

$1,000 PER CARAT.

▶ What's the weirdest **ITEM OF VALUE** you have in your bedroom?

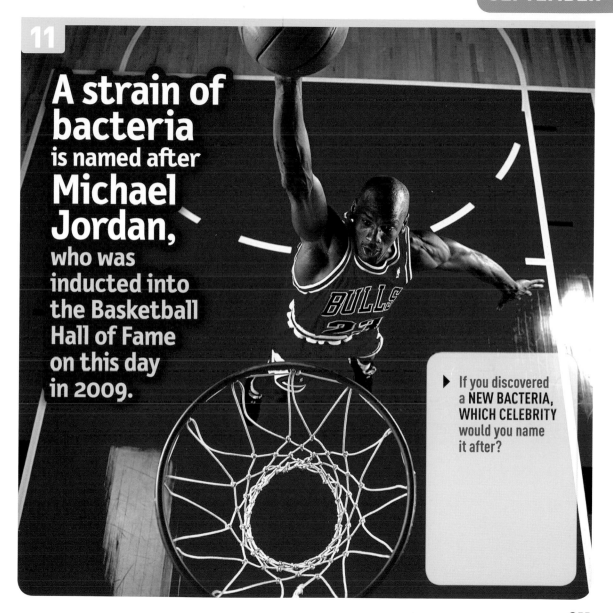

11

A strain of bacteria is named after **Michael Jordan,** who was inducted into the Basketball Hall of Fame on this day in 2009.

▶ If you discovered a **NEW BACTERIA, WHICH CELEBRITY** would you name it after?

BULLS

▶ Using words that begin with the letter *J*, create new **NICKNAMES** for each member of your family.

Four-time Olympic gold medalist JAMES CLEVELAND OWENS was called "J. C." by his family. His teacher misheard the name, called him "JESSE," and it stuck.

13 TODAY IS — FORTUNE COOKIE DAY

Fortune cookies were invented in Japan, not China.

▶ Make up a **FORTUNE** for **YOURSELF.**

14

ON THIS DAY IN 1814, FRANCIS SCOTT KEY WROTE THE U.S. NATIONAL ANTHEM, "**THE STAR-SPANGLED BANNER,**" ON THE BACK OF A LETTER.

▶ Make up a **NEW PATRIOTIC SONG.** Write the first line here.

For one year in 1752, the United Kingdom

REMOVED 11 DAYS

from the month of September.

▶ What month would you **SHORTEN** by 11 **DAYS?**

16

▶ When was the last time you **GOT LOST?**

On this day in 1620, THE *MAYFLOWER* set sail from England, but their destination was *not Massachusetts.*
IT WAS VIRGINIA. (Bad weather blew them off course.)

215

Take the word "September" and see how many **NEW WORDS** you can make from its nine letters.

September, the
NINTH MONTH,
is the only one with the same number of letters in its name as its place in the sequence of months.

18

▶ QUIZ! Which one of these goddesses is **NOT** a moon goddess?
A. Luna (Rome)
B. Chang'e (China)
C. Isis (Egypt)
D. Artemis (Greece)

Answer: C

The **FULL MOON** closest to the autumnal equinox is called the **HARVEST MOON** because farmers use its light **TO COMPLETE THE HARVEST.**

19

TODAY IS — TALK LIKE A PIRATE DAY

▶ Write a sentence in **PIRATE-SPEAK** here.

A **cannon** hauled up from the wreck of Blackbeard's pirate ship weighed **3,000 pounds!** (1,360 kg)

20

Each September, the United States' North Carolina Museum of Natural Sciences celebrates BugFest with "entomophagy" or

bug-eating.

▶ Would you ever **EAT A BUG?** What kind?

Competitors in the World Gurning Championship, held each September in England, win by making the

ugliest face possible.

▶ Describe the **UGLIEST FACE** you can make.

21

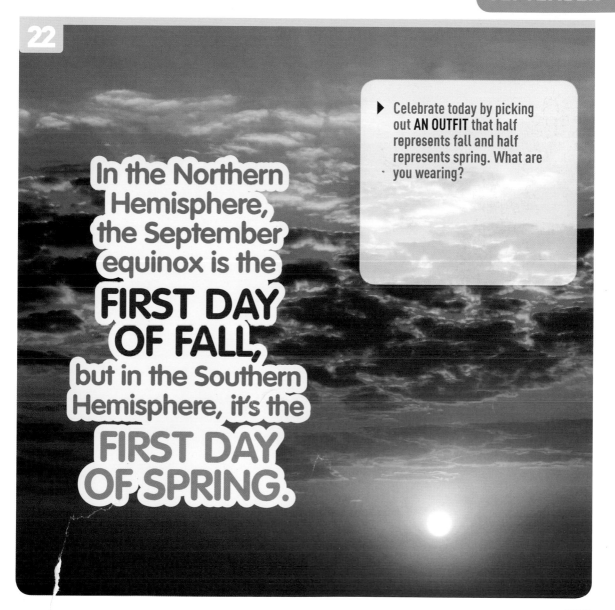

22

In the Northern Hemisphere, the September equinox is the **FIRST DAY OF FALL,** but in the Southern Hemisphere, it's the **FIRST DAY OF SPRING.**

▶ Celebrate today by picking out **AN OUTFIT** that half represents fall and half represents spring. What are you wearing?

23

▶ If you **DISCOVERED A PLANET,** what would you name it? Write down your top five candidates here.

The planet Neptune, discovered on this day in 1846 by a German astronomer, has the strongest winds in the solar system, topping out at 1,500 miles an hour. (2,414 kph)

24

PUPPETEER JIM HENSON created KERMIT THE FROG out of his MOM'S COAT and two PING-PONG BALLS.

HAPPY BIRTHDAY · JIM HENSON

▶ Draw your **FAVORITE MUPPET** here or design your own.

25

THE ANGLO-SAXONS CALLED SEPTEMBER **GERSTMONATH,** OR **"BARLEY MONTH."**

▶ Give September a **NEW NAME.**

26

TENNIS SUPERSTAR **SERENA WILLIAMS** BEGAN PLAYING TENNIS AT AGE **THREE.**

▶ How many times can you **BOUNCE A TENNIS BALL** on a racket without dropping the ball?

27

In 1989, Jeffrey Perkovich and Peter DeBernardi became the first team to survive going over Niagara Falls in a barrel together.

▶ What's the **MOST DARING** thing you've ever done?

29

SEPTEMBER IS ALL-AMERICAN BREAKFAST MONTH.

The average American eats

267 eggs

for breakfast each year.

▶ **QUIZ!** What is the average number of eggs **ONE HEN** lays in a year?
A. 67
B. 259
C. 1,920
D. 714

Answer: B

30

New York Yankee **BABE RUTH,** who hit his 60th home run of the season on this day in 1927, was nicknamed **THE BAMBINO,** Italian for "baby boy."

▶ What **STRANGE NICKNAMES** do you and your friends have for each other? List them here.

OCTOBER

NASA

NASA scientists have found **OPAL**, one of October's birthstones, **ON MARS.**

▶ What are three other things you'd like to FIND ON MARS?

October is American Cheese Month.

Scientists once used a 3-D printer loaded with cheese instead of ink to print a tiny, edible space shuttle.

▶ Make a **CHEESE SCULPTURE.** Glue a picture of it here.

3

The red color in
fall leaves
protects
them like a
sunscreen.

▶ Go outside and **COLLECT** as many red **LEAVES** of different shades, shapes, and sizes as you can. Write down here how they are different and how they are alike.

4 **October** is a good month to look outdoors for **FUNGI,** like mushrooms. **FUNGI** are more closely related to animals than plants.

(But don't eat any mushrooms you find outside!)

▶ **MAKE UP A JOKE** about mushrooms. Write it below.

▶ What other things would you not be surprised to find growing right **UNDER YOUR FEET?**

5 There's a fungus the size of **1,665 football fields** growing in eastern Oregon, U.S.A.

6

Stinkhorn, bearded tooth, and hen of the woods are all types of **FUNGI.**

▶ Make up three more weird **MUSHROOM NAMES.**

231

7

October is National Popcorn Poppin' Month in the United States.

Hundreds of years ago, people ate popcorn for breakfast as a cereal.

▶ Try eating **POPCORN WITH MILK** for breakfast one morning. Write down your thoughts about it here.

8

R.L. STINE

Author of the spooky Goosebumps series, R.L. Stine got his start writing joke books.

▶ What's the **SCARIEST PLACE** you've ever been?

9

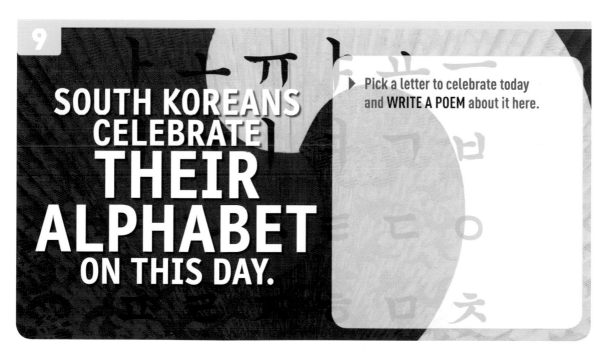

SOUTH KOREANS CELEBRATE THEIR ALPHABET ON THIS DAY.

▶ Pick a letter to celebrate today and **WRITE A POEM** about it here.

10

BONZA BOTTLER DAY CELEBRATES THE DAY OF THE MONTH THAT MATCHES IT IN NUMBER:

January 1st (1/1), February 2nd (2/2), March 3rd (3/3) ...

▶ **QUIZ!** The Bonza Bottler Day **MASCOT** is a:
A. juggling wombat
B. tap-dancing zebra
C. dancing groundhog

Answer: C.

11 TODAY IS   **INTERNATIONAL MIGRATORY BIRD DAY!** (Caribbean nations)

One of the Caribbean's **flyover birds,** the blackpoll warbler, nearly **doubles its weight** before flying south for the winter.

▶ What would you eat if you needed to **DOUBLE YOUR WEIGHT?**

12

The movie credits at the end of *Harry Potter and the Goblet of Fire* include the statement:

"No dragons were harmed in the making of this movie."

▶ In a **MOVIE ABOUT YOUR LIFE,** what would the final line of dialogue be?

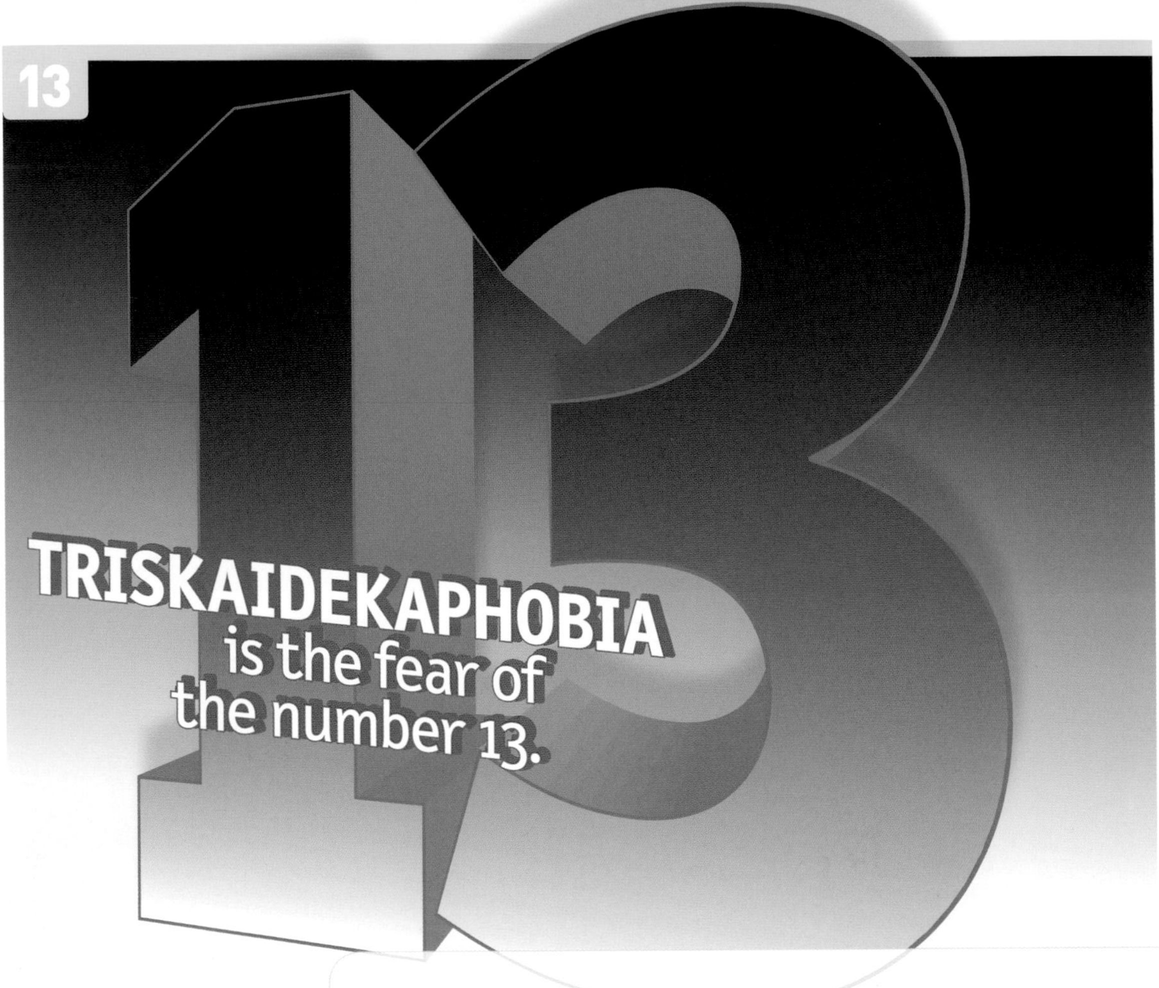

TRISKAIDEKAPHOBIA is the fear of the number 13.

▶ **PICK A NUMBER** and create a name for **THE FEAR OF IT.**

14 October is National Pizza Month in the United States. Shrimp and potato with pumpkin seed and raisin crust is a popular South Korean–style pizza.

▶ What's the **WEIRDEST PIZZA** you've ever eaten?

15 Mozzarella cheese was originally made from water buffalo milk, not cow's milk.

▶ Have you **EVER TRIED** buffalo mozzarella? Would you?

Across England this month, people **TOSS MANGOLDS** —a large vegetable—while **STANDING IN A BUCKET,** as part of a sport known as **MANGOLD HURLING.**

▶ Find a bucket, stand in it, and **THROW A VEGETABLE** (carefully). Record the distance it traveled here.

Bears in the Northern Hemisphere begin hibernation this month.

Hibernating bears don't poop.

18

During hibernation, some black bears' **heart rates drop** from 55 to just 9 beats a minute.

▶ If YOU COULD HIBERNATE through one season, which would it be and why?

Contestants race
**FUZZY
CATERPILLARS**
up strings at the
Woolly Worm Festival
in Banner Elk,
North Carolina, U.S.A.,
each October.
The colors of
the **WINNING
CATERPILLAR**
are said to forecast
the forthcoming
winter weather.

▶ Do you have any **WEIRD TRICKS** for **FORECASTING** weather?

20

The world's largest
pumpkin
weighed more than a
horse.

▶ What kind of
**WEIRD WORLD
RECORD** would
you like to set?

The world record for most apples bobbed in a minute is 34.

> **BOB FOR APPLES** and record how many you can catch in one minute.

Draw a picture of **YOUR FAVORITE FRUIT** as a **FLOWER**.

22

Apples are members of the rose family.

NATIONAL MOLE DAY

NATIONAL MOLE DAY
doesn't honor the animal but celebrates the mole, a basic measuring unit used in chemistry.

▶ Illustrate and name **A MASCOT** for National Mole Day.

24

Children sometimes **grow new fingertips** if they've been cut off accidentally.

▶ If you had the ability to **GROW A NEW BODY PART,** what would it be and why?

25

12,000 years ago, the La Brea Tar Pits
in Los Angeles, California, U.S.A., trapped animals as big as cows in less than 2 inches of tar!

(5 cm)

▶ What's the weirdest thing you've ever seen COME UP from UNDERGROUND?

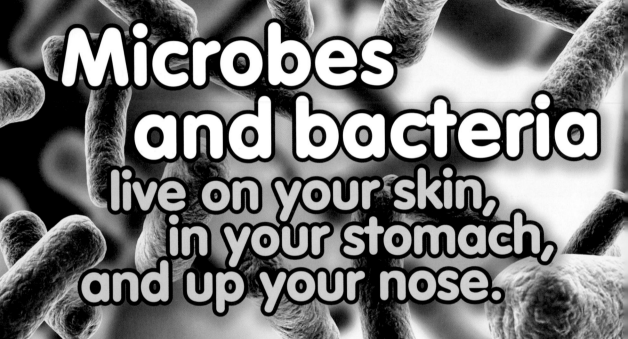

Microbes
and bacteria
live on your skin,
in your stomach,
and up your nose.

▶ If **YOU WERE A MICROBE,** where would you like to live and why?

27

A scientific study of people's belly buttons found **2,368** **different types** of bacteria living inside.

▶ Write a five-line POEM ABOUT BELLY BUTTONS.

28

THE WORD **"SINISTER"** MEANS **"LEFT-HAND"** IN LATIN.

▶ If you're right-handed, use your **LEFT HAND** to write your name here. If you're left-handed, write your name with your **RIGHT HAND**.

29

People sleep less on full-moon nights, even in windowless rooms.

▶ Write down three weird things a
FULL MOON might **MAKE PEOPLE DO.**

30 Every October, millions
of Mexican free-tailed
bats fly from a single cave
in Texas, U.S.A., to their
winter home in Mexico
1,000 miles away.
(1,609 km)

31

 TODAY IS · HALLOWEEN

People used to carve jack-o'-lanterns from turnips.

▶ Sketch a design that could be **CARVED ON A TURNIP.**

▶ Create a map of made-up bat **NEIGHBORHOODS** inside the cave.

249

NOVEMBER

1

Contestants have hurled pumpkins more than half a mile (0.8 km) at the **WORLD CHAMPIONSHIP PUNKIN CHUNKIN COMPETITION,** held every November in Delaware, U.S.A. The record stands at 4,483 feet! (1,366 m)

▶ Write down three creative ways to **SMASH A PUMPKIN.**

2

IT'S INTERNATIONAL DRUM MONTH.

The world record for longest drum roll is 8 hours 1 minute and 17 seconds.

▶ What is something you think you could do for **8 HOURS STRAIGHT?**

3 TODAY IS SANDWICH DAY

Legend has it that ...

JOHN MONTAGU, 4TH EARL OF SANDWICH, invented the sandwich in the 18th century while playing games for 24 hours and eating nothing but cold beef between toast.

▶ List the ingredients for **the WEIRDEST SANDWICH** you can think of.

4

In November 1977,
an 8-year-old
ran the New York City
Marathon—
26.2 miles—
in just over **(42.2 km)**
3 hours.

▶ Using a map, find a location that
is about **26 MILES** from your
house. How long do you think it
would take to **RUN THERE?**

▶ See how long you can **HOP ON ONE LEG** while it's **TIED** to a friend's leg. Record your time here.

5 **Five men once ran a marathon while tied together at the waist.**

6

In 1990, 80,000 pairs of Nike tennis shoes were lost at sea.

▶ What's one thing you would **WANT 80,000 OF?**

255

7

In early November, people carry

flaming tar barrels

through the streets of Ottery St. Mary, England.

▶ Describe the weirdest thing you've ever seen **PASS THROUGH** your **HOMETOWN**.

At the World Beard and Moustache Championships, held every two years in November, contestants compete in 18 categories, including Imperial Moustache, Fu Manchu, and Amish Beard.

▶ Draw a new design for a **MUSTACHE** and give it a **FANCY NAME**.

9 November is also known as Movember, a month when "mos," or mustaches, are grown to raise money for men's health issues.

▶ List all 12 months and **ASSIGN** each of them a specific **HAIRSTYLE**.

▶ Sketch how you would wear **YOUR MUSTACHE** if it were 14 FEET LONG.

10

THE LONGEST MUSTACHE IN THE WORLD MEASURED MORE THAN

14 FEET.
(4 M)

11

A key ingredient in some insect repellents comes from **chrysanthemums,**

November's **birth flower.**

November is National Novel Writing Month.

12 The 154-page novel **Gadsby,** by Ernest Vincent Wright, doesn't contain a single word with the letter *e*.

▶ In one minute, see how many words you can list that **DON'T CONTAIN THE LETTER *E*.**

13 Harry Potter author **J.K. Rowling**'s real name is Joanne Rowling. She doesn't really have a **middle name.**

▶ Give **YOURSELF a PEN NAME.**

259

14

HELLO, MY NAME IS

In the United States, **AUTUMN** is the most popular seasonal name for babies; Spring is the least popular.

▶ Assign a **SEASONAL NAME** to everyone who lives in your household.

15

 TODAY IS NATIONAL CLEAN OUT YOUR REFRIGERATOR DAY

In 1930, **Albert Einstein** and fellow physicist **Leo Szilard** invented a refrigerator that required *no electricity.*

▶ What's the **WEIRDEST** thing you've ever found **IN YOUR FRIDGE?**

16 **Goober** is another name for peanut. It also means **a foolish person.**

▶ Write a short poem or song about a **FOOLISH PEANUT.**

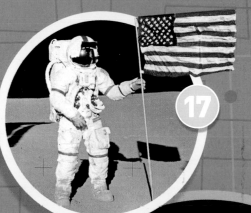

17

Astronaut ALAN SHEPARD brought A PEANUT with him to the moon in 1971.

▶ Pretend you're **PACKING FOR THE MOON.** Make a list of three necessary items here.

▶ What are some unusual foods that you would try with **PEANUT BUTTER?**

18 At a diner in Cleveland, Ohio, U.S.A., you can get a **PEANUTBURGER,** a hamburger slathered in peanut butter!

19

TODAY IS **WORLD TOILET DAY**

▶ **QUIZ!** Which of the
following is not
SLANG FOR "TOILET"?
A. breem
B. bog
C. head

Answer: A

The U.S. president's home,
the White House, has
35 TOILETS.

20

TODAY IS

UNIVERSAL CHILDREN'S DAY and also ABSURDITY DAY

Young people and young goats are both called **KIDS.**

▶ Create **THREE NEW WORDS** for "children" and "young goats."

21 *The seventh largest lake on Earth, Lake Vostok, is* **2.3 miles** (3.7 km) *beneath Antarctica's ice.*

▶ Describe three new **BIZARRE ORGANISMS** scientists might find living in Lake Vostok.

▸ Draw a picture of a **BLEEDING** iceberg.

22 There's a **glacier** in Antarctica that looks like it's **bleeding;** but it's really just leaking iron-rich red water.

▸ If you could have any **EXTINCT CREATURE** for a **PET**, which would you choose and why?

23 Scientists successfully regrew moss that had been trapped **under a glacier** for centuries.

24

On this day in 1973, Germany imposed a speed limit on its national highway system. Today, though, most of its highways have NO SPEED LIMIT.

▶ Draw a
TRAFFIC SIGN
that you
might see on
a highway
that has no
speed limit.

25

Held in November, Thailand's

Monkey Buffet Festival

is a giant feast for the country's monkeys.

▶ **CREATE A MENU** for the Monkey Buffet Festival.

26 The **giant balloons** in the Macy's Thanksgiving Day Parade used to be **released** at the end of the route.

▶ Describe how you would **RETURN** one of these **BALLOONS** to its owner if you found it.

The record for **most balloons** inflated by a nose in 3 minutes is **23.**

27

▶ **HOW MANY BUBBLES** can you blow and pop in one minute? Record your number here.

PARK CENTRAL HOTEL

28

There were **no forks** at the first Thanksgiving in 1621.

▶ If you had to **EAT WITH** only one **UTENSIL** for the rest of your life, which would you choose?

29

Sastrugi, sun cups, and megadunes are all types of

SNOW

formations.

▶ Pretend you've just discovered a
NEW TYPE OF SNOW.
Name and describe it here.

30

In the mountains, you can find bright pink "watermelon snow," which gets its color and watermelon smell from tiny algae.

▶ **WHICH FOOD** would you most like snow to **TASTE LIKE?**

DECEMBER

The first candy canes did not have stripes.

1

▶ Draw a picture of **YOUR OWN CANDY CANE** design here. What colors would you use? Describe its flavors.

2

In Massachusetts, U.S.A., it is illegal to drive a **horse-drawn sleigh** with fewer than **three bells** on it.

▶ Write down as many **SONGS** as you can that mention **BELLS**.

3

QUIZ! WHICH of these words doesn't have anything to do with the NUMBER 10?
A. decathlon
B. decagon
C. decorate

Answer: C

December is based on the Latin word for **"ten"** because it used to be **the tenth month** of the year.

4

First published on this day, the U.K.'s *Observer* has been printing a Sunday newspaper for more than 220 years!

▶ WRITE SOME HEADLINES about weird things that have happened in your life.

277

5

HAPPY BIRTHDAY WALT DISNEY

WALT DISNEY was the voice of MICKEY MOUSE for 20 years.

▶ Have a best **CARTOON VOICE** contest with your friends. Write down the winners and what characters they imitated.

▶ If you could **CHANGE YOUR LAST NAME,** what would you change it to? Why?

6

Walt Disney's ancestors changed their last name from D'ISIGNY to DISNEY when they emigrated from France to England.

7 Walt Disney was an AMBULANCE DRIVER during WWI.

▶ What do you think a **DISNEY-INSPIRED** ambulance would look like? Draw one here.

⑧ TURQUOISE—

the official gemstone of December—is named after **TURKEY,** because that is where it was **FIRST DISCOVERED.**

▶ Spin a globe, pick a country, and come up with a **NEW GEM.** Name your jewel after the country and draw a picture of it here.

▶ If you could **BAN** any type of **CLOTHING,** which would you choose?

9 # THE MAYA RULED THAT NO ONE WAS ALLOWED TO WEAR TURQUOISE, because it was used as an offering to THE GODS.

December is National Read a New Book Month.

In the 16th century, the **world's best-selling book** was about TEACHING CHILDREN GOOD MANNERS.

▶ Make up three new **WACKY RULES** for **MANNERS**.

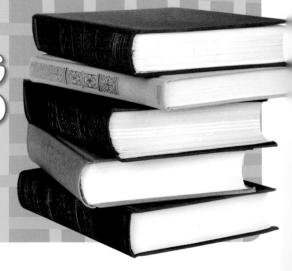

11

In Ukraine, it's customary to decorate your Christmas tree with **spiderwebs.**

▶ What is the weirdest **HOLIDAY DECORATION** that your family puts up each year?

283

POINSETTIA FLOWERS are the tiny yellow structures in the center of the plant. THE RED "PETALS" are actually specialized leaves called BRACTS.

▶ **DESCRIBE** a time when you were **SURPRISED** to find out something was not what you thought it was.

13

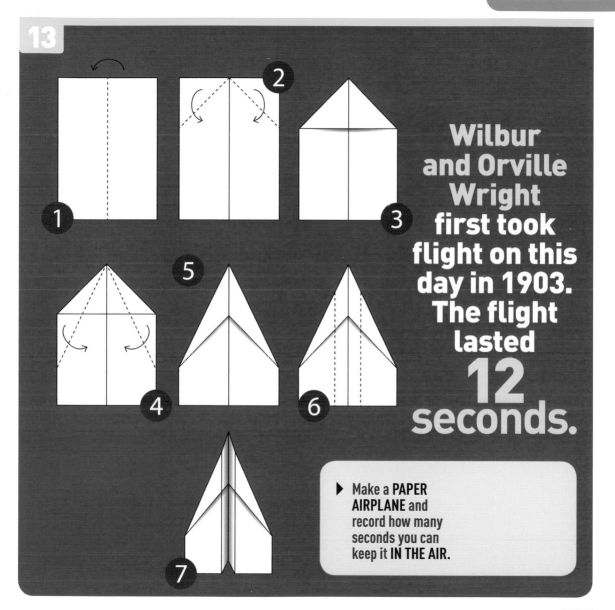

Wilbur and Orville Wright first took flight on this day in 1903. The flight lasted **12 seconds.**

▶ Make a **PAPER AIRPLANE** and record how many seconds you can keep it **IN THE AIR.**

14

Howler monkeys
are so loud they can be heard from
three miles
(5 km) **away.**

▶ Get together with some friends and listen to see how **FAR AWAY** you can hear each other howl. Record who has the **LOUDEST HOWL** here.

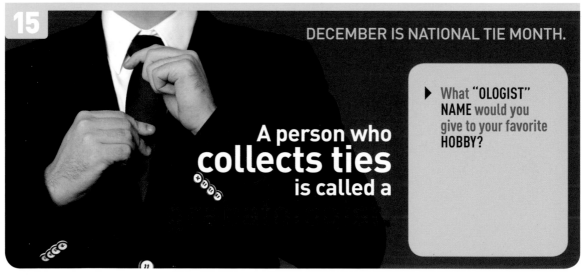

15

DECEMBER IS NATIONAL TIE MONTH.

A person who
collects ties
is called a

▶ What "**OLOGIST**" **NAME** would you give to your favorite **HOBBY**?

TODAY IS NATIONAL CHOCOLATE-COVERED ANYTHING DAY

16 Aztec emperor **Moctezuma** reportedly drank 50 cups of chocolate per day.

▶ What's your **FAVORITE WAY** to drink **HOT COCOA?**

17

▶ Experiment: **HOW MANY** Hershey's Kisses do you think are in one bag? **TAKE GUESSES** from all your family members, write them down here, then count the Kisses to see who is closest!

Side by side, all the **Hershey's Kisses** produced in a year would stretch in a line more than **300,000** miles long.

(482,800 km)

TODAY IS BAKE COOKIES DAY

THE FIRST COOKIES WERE BELIEVED TO HAVE BEEN INVENTED IN ANCIENT IRAN!

▶ What's the **WEIRDEST** kind of **COOKIE** you've ever eaten?

19

"Dreidel" comes from the German verb *dreihen*, which means to

SPIN.

SHIN HEY

▶ Get together with **SOME FRIENDS** and count how many times you can each **SPIN AROUND** in 30 seconds. Write down the winner here.

20

QUIZ! Which of the following words is not a **SYNONYM FOR "STILL"**?
A. motionless
B. silent
C. couched

Answer: C.

"Solstice"

comes from the term

"sun stands still" *in Latin.*

21

Winter solstice is the

shortest
day *of the year*
in the Northern Hemisphere.

▶ If you had to **ELIMINATE** one daily **ACTIVITY** from your routine, what would it be?

289

NATIONAL HAIKU POETRY DAY

HAIKU
IS A TYPE OF JAPANESE POEM THAT HAS ONLY 17 SYLLABLES.
TRADITION SAYS THAT'S THE IDEAL NUMBER TO UTTER IN ONE BREATH.

▶ Write **YOUR OWN HAIKU** here about something weird that happened to you. The first line should have five syllables, the second seven, and the third five.

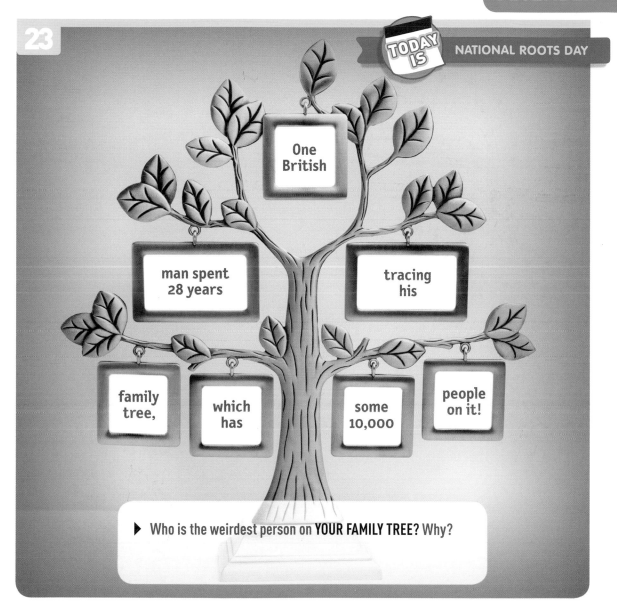

23

TODAY IS NATIONAL ROOTS DAY

One British

man spent 28 years

tracing his

family tree,

which has

some 10,000

people on it!

▶ Who is the weirdest person on **YOUR FAMILY TREE?** Why?

24

The first artificial Christmas tree was made out of **GOOSE FEATHERS** that were **DYED GREEN.**

▶ Draw a picture of you **DECORATING A GOOSE** with green feathers.

▶ If you had to update this song, **WHAT GIFTS** would you replace? Write down your ideas for each of the 12 days.

25

If you added up all the gifts in *"THE 12 DAYS OF CHRISTMAS,"* you would have **364 GIFTS.**

No one really knows how

BOXING DAY

—a holiday celebrated today in Canada, Great Britain, Australia, and New Zealand—actually began.

▶ Make up two sentences about the **ORIGIN** of Boxing Day.

27

KWANZAA

means "fresh fruits" in Swahili.

▶ **QUIZ!** Which of these foods is **NOT A FRUIT?**
a. eggplant
b. tomato
c. carrot
d. olive

Answer: C

28

▶ What **REAL-LIFE PEOPLE** would you have as the king, queen, and jack?

The face cards in a deck used to represent

real royalty

—like Julius Caesar, Charlemagne, and Alexander the Great.

29 Texas

was an independent nation until it became a state on this day in **1845.**

▶ If you ruled **YOUR OWN COUNTRY,** what would you call it?

30

Texas comes from the Hasinai Indian word *tejas,* **which means "friends".**

▶ Use these words for "friend" from other languages to create a name for a **NEW STATE:** *Freund* (German), *amigo* (Spanish), *ami* (French), *arkadaş* (Turkish), *rafiki* (Swahili), *přítel* (Czech).

31

2,000 pounds
(900 kg)
of confetti are dropped on Times Square every New Year's Eve.

▶ Grab your friends and dress up in your weirdest **NEW YEAR'S EVE ATTIRE.** Take a picture and place it on this page.

MAPPY NEW YEAR!

CHEVROLET

Budweiser
HAPPY NEW YEAR

NEW YORK

FACTFINDER

The National Geographic Society is one of the world's largest nonprofit scientific and educational organizations. Founded in 1888 to "increase and diffuse geographic knowledge," the Society works to inspire people to care about the planet. National Geographic reflects the world through its magazines, television programs, films, music and radio, books, DVDs, maps, exhibitions, live events, school publishing programs, interactive media and merchandise. *National Geographic* magazine, the Society's official journal, published in English and 33 local-language editions, is read by more than 38 million people each month. The National Geographic Channel reaches 320 million households in 34 languages in 166 countries. National Geographic Digital Media receives more than 15 million visitors a month. National Geographic has funded more than 9,400 scientific research, conservation and exploration projects and supports an education program promoting geography literacy.

For more information, please call
1-800-NGS LINE (647-5463) or
write to the following address:
National Geographic Society
1145 17th Street N.W.
Washington, D.C. 20036-4688 U.S.A.

Published by the National Geographic Society
Gary E. Knell, *President and Chief Executive Officer*
John M. Fahey, *Chairman of the Board*
Declan Moore, *Executive Vice President; President, Publishing and Travel*
Melina Gerosa Bellows, *Publisher; Chief Creative Officer, Books, Kids, and Family*

Prepared by the Book Division
Hector Sierra, *Senior Vice President and General Manager*
Nancy Laties Feresten, *Senior Vice President, Kids Publishing and Media*
Jay Sumner, *Director of Photography, Kids Publishing*
Jennifer Emmett, *Vice President, Editorial Director, Kids Books*
Eva Absher-Schantz, *Design Director, Kids Publishing and Media*
R. Gary Colbert, *Production Director*
Jennifer A. Thornton, *Director of Managing Editorial*

Staff for This Book
Becky Baines, *Senior Editor*
Amy Briggs, *Project Manager*
Julide Obuz Dengel, *Art Director*
Hillary Leo, *Photo Editor*
Chad Tomlinson, *Designer*
Jeannette Kimmel, Emily Krieger, Meg Weaver *Researchers*
Ariane Szu-Tu, *Editorial Assistant*
Paige Towler, *Special Projects Assistant*
Callie Broaddus, *Design Production Assistant*
Margaret Leist, *Photo Assistant*
Grace Hill, *Associate Managing Editor*
Mike O'Connor, *Production Editor*
Lewis R. Bassford, *Production Manager*
Susan Borke, *Legal and Business Affairs*

Production Services
Phillip L. Schlosser, *Senior Vice President*
Chris Brown, *Vice President, NG Book Manufacturing*
George Bounelis, *Senior Production Manager*
Nicole Elliott, *Director of Production*
Rachel Faulise, *Manager*
Robert L. Barr, *Manager*

HOW WEIRD (but true) R U?

Now it's time to see where kids coast to coast—and YOU!—measure up on the Weird-o-Meter!

Can you do a cartwheel?

How many stuffed animals live in your room with you?

Is your second toe bigger than your big toe?

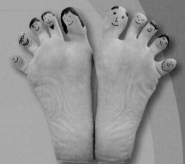

More than 100 questions test ARE YOU NORMAL?—or not!

STANDARD

A LITTLE WACKY

WEIRD

NORMAL

ONE OF A KIND

For 67 percent of kids, their big toe IS their big toe.

42 percent of kids have 20 stuffed animals or more!

Only 1 in 3 kids can do a decent cartwheel.

ANSWERS:

NATIONAL GEOGRAPHIC KIDS

ARE YOU "NORMAL"? 2
BY MARK SHULMAN

MORE THAN 100 QUESTIONS THAT WILL TEST YOUR WEIRDNESS

© 2014 National Geographic Society

AVAILABLE WHEREVER BOOKS ARE SOLD
and at nationalgeographic.com/books

Like us on Facebook: Nat Geo Books
Follow us on Twitter: @NatGeoBooks

NATIONAL GEOGRAPHIC KiDS